Mountain
Moving
Faith

Mountain Moving
Faith

Kenneth E. Hagin

29 28 27 26 25 24 23   21 20 19 18 17 16 15

Mountain-Moving Faith
ISBN-13: 978-0-89276-522-5
ISBN-10: 0-89276-522-4

In the U.S. write:
Kenneth Hagin Ministries
P.O. Box 50126
Tulsa, OK 74150-0126
1-888-28-FAITH
rhema.org

In Canada write:
Kenneth Hagin Ministries of Canada
P.O. Box 335, Station D
Etobicoke (Toronto), Ontario
Canada M9A 4X3
1-866-70-RHEMA
rhemacanada.org

Contents

Chapter One

Every Believer Has Faith

You just can't talk about the subject of faith without getting into Mark chapter 11, because in this passage of scripture are the most amazing, thrilling, wonderful statements on the subject of faith that ever fell from the lips of the Master.

MARK 11:22–26

22 And Jesus answering saith unto them [the disciples], Have faith in God.

23 For verily I say unto you, That whosoever shall say unto this mountain, Be thou removed, and be thou cast into the sea; and shall not doubt in his heart, but shall believe that those things which he saith shall come to pass; he shall have whatsoever he saith.

24 Therefore I say unto you, What things soever ye desire, when ye pray, believe that ye receive them, and ye shall have them.

25 And when ye stand praying, forgive, if ye have ought against any: that your Father also which is in heaven may forgive you your trespasses.

26 But if ye do not forgive, neither will your Father which is in heaven forgive your trespasses.

What I've done in this book is to sum up the seven most important things on the subject of faith. And the first most important fact about faith is that every believer has a measure of the God-kind of faith.

I used to hold quite lengthy meetings. We would hold meetings for local churches, and sometimes we would put on our own meetings.

Back in those days, I'd never accept an invitation for less than three weeks. And then many times we'd stay four to eight weeks in one place. One time we stayed nine weeks. We held two services a day, five days a week.

Of course, when we stayed that long—anywhere from four to nine weeks—we had plenty of time to go into detail on the subject of faith and just sort of turn over every stone and look under every rock. For example, we'd talk about things like, "If your faith is not working, why isn't it working?" We'd deal with this and other areas of faith, and we'd call it a "Faith Clinic."

But when you're in a meeting just a week with the people, and you have only five or six services, you've got to condense your teaching and give it to them in capsule form. In other words, you give them the most important points on the subject of faith.

So in this book, I'll get you headed in the right direction. Then you continue to feed along the line of faith yourself.

Notice Mark 11:22 of our text: *"And Jesus answering saith unto them, Have faith in God."* The margin of the *King James* translation reads that Jesus said, "Have the faith *of* God."

Another translation reads (in fact, Greek scholars tell us it is a literal translation): "Have the God-kind of faith." Literally, Jesus actually said, "Have the God-kind of faith"!

If you didn't know a thing in the world about the Greek language, you could still readily see that's a correct translation, for Jesus had just demonstrated to the disciples that He had that kind of faith—the God-kind of faith.

MARK 11:12–14, 20–22
12 And on the morrow, when they were come from Bethany, he was hungry:
13 And seeing a fig tree afar off having leaves, he came, if haply he might find any thing thereon: and when he came to it, he found nothing but leaves; for the time of figs was not yet.

14 And Jesus answered and said unto it, No man eat fruit of thee hereafter for ever. And his disciples heard it. . . .

20 And in the morning, as they passed by, they saw the fig tree dried up from the roots.

21 And Peter calling to remembrance saith unto him, Master, behold, the fig tree which thou cursedst is withered away.

22 And Jesus answering saith unto them, Have faith in God [or Have the God-kind of faith].

Then in verse 23, Jesus goes on to describe or to define the God-kind of faith.

MARK 11:23

23 For verily I say unto you, That whosoever shall SAY unto this mountain, Be thou removed, and be thou cast into the sea; and shall not DOUBT in his heart, but shall BELIEVE that those things which he SAITH shall come to pass; he shall have whatsoever he SAITH.

The God-kind of faith is the kind of faith in which a person believes in his heart, and then he says with his mouth what he believes in his heart. And Jesus said, "When that happens, it'll come to pass."

That's the same kind of faith God used to create the worlds in the beginning. He simply believed that what He said would come to pass, so He said, "Let there be an earth." And there was an earth. Then He said, "Let the animals be." And they became!

Everything that's here—the sun, the moon, the stars—God created by simply speaking them into existence and believing that what He said would come to pass. He said it, and it came to pass!

Now everything that's here, except man, came that way. All of creation came into being because God spoke them into being. That is the God-kind of faith.

Don't Pray for Faith

You see, in Mark 11:12–21, Jesus had just demonstrated that He had that kind of faith—the same kind of faith that God used to create the worlds in the beginning. Then He said to the disciples, "*You*, have the God-kind of faith"!

Now most folks would say, "That's what I *want*, and I'm praying that God will give it to me." Well, if that's what you're doing, you're wasting your time. Actually, it would do no more good to pray that God would give you faith than it would be for you to twiddle your thumbs and say, "Twinkle, twinkle, little star, how I wonder what you are"!

You see, much of our praying is lost motion and wasted time, because *every* believer already has a measure of this kind of faith. You don't have to *get* it; you've already *got* it, praise God! You have a measure of this God-kind of faith!

So my first thought to you is this: This faith Jesus is talking about in Mark chapter 11 is the God-kind of faith, and every believer already has a measure of this kind of faith. You don't have to get it; you don't have to pray for it; you don't have to fast for it; and you don't have to promise to do better and be good in order to get it. You already *have* it! I can prove that by the Bible.

ROMANS 12:3

3 For I say, through the grace given unto me, to every man that is among you, not to think of himself more highly than he ought to think; but to think soberly, according as GOD HATH DEALT TO EVERY MAN THE MEASURE OF FAITH.

I want to call your attention to the fact that in this verse, Paul is not writing to sinners, or the world, but to *believers*—to Christians. He said, "I say to every man that is among *you*," not every man that is in the world.

Some people just try to find contradictions in the Bible. There aren't any contradictions in the Bible. But if you take verses out of their setting, there may seem to be contradictions.

For example, in Paul's second letter to the Thessalonians, he made this statement: *"all men HAVE NOT FAITH"* (2 Thess. 3:2). Yet here in Romans 12:3, Paul said, *"according as God hath dealt TO EVERY MAN THE MEASURE OF FAITH."*

Now if you just looked at those two statements (and, really, each statement is just *part* of a verse taken out of its setting), they would seem to contradict each other. The same writer says one thing in one verse and something that seems completely different in another verse. Some folks would say, "Then it must not be inspired of God. It just shows up Paul's confusion."

In Second Thessalonians 3:2, Paul said, *"all men have not faith."* And in Romans 12:3, he said that *every* man has the measure of faith. But if you'll read the entire verse of Second Thessalonians 3:2, you can see that Paul is speaking here of *ungodly* men, not believers. He said, *"And that we may be delivered from unreasonable and WICKED men: for all men have not faith."*

Paul was talking about folks in the world—ungodly men—people without God. All men in the world do not have faith; that is, they don't have the God-kind of faith. They may have a natural human faith, or a head faith. But they don't have the God-kind of faith.

But all believers *do* have the God-kind of faith! Paul said, *"For I say, through the grace given unto me, TO EVERY MAN THAT IS AMONG YOU . . . according as God hath dealt to EVERY MAN the measure of faith"* (Rom. 12:3). You see, all believers have faith.

Here's where a lot of believers make a mistake. They say, "My trouble is, I don't have any faith." I always say to them, "Well, why don't you get saved then, because *saved* people have faith! You can't be saved without having faith."

EPHESIANS 2:8
8 For by grace are ye saved THROUGH FAITH; and that not of yourselves: it is the gift of God.

I tell folks, "If you really don't have faith, then you're not saved. What you need to do is get saved, and that will solve your problem of not having faith."

The truth about the matter is, all believers have faith. The Bible says so. But many believers don't recognize it or realize it, and they're not *using* their faith.

Use the Faith You Have

Years ago, a woman came rushing up to me after one meeting and said, "Brother Hagin, I want you to pray for me."

"What for, Sister?" I answered.

She said, "I want you to pray that I'll have faith. I need healing for my body." In other words, she implied that she didn't have faith to receive healing.

"I'm not going to do it," I said.

It startled the woman when I said that to her. I don't think anybody had ever talked to her like that before.

I said that to get her attention, and I got it! Many times, you've got to get people's attention before you can help them.

When I said that to the woman, she said, "You're really not going to pray?"

I said, "No, ma'am. I'm not."

Again she said, "You're really not?"

I said, "I'm really not. I'm not going to pray one lick. I'm not going to pray one time that you'll have faith."

"Well," she said, "I sure do need healing."

I said to her, "Aren't you a believer, Sister?"

"Oh, why, of course I am!" she said.

I said, "Well, who ever heard of a believer who doesn't believe? How could you be a believer without believing?"

I continued: "There's no use for me to pray that you'll have faith. You *have* faith. Use the faith you have."

The very next night this woman was in the healing line. When I got to her, I said, "Well, I see you've come." She had come for her healing. The night before she wanted me to pray that she'd have faith so she could receive her healing. But now she was acting on the faith she already had.

"Yeah," she said, "I've come, and I'll be healed too. Just lay your hands on me."

She decided to use her faith!

I laid hands on her for her healing, and when I did, I also perceived that she did not have the fullness of the Spirit. That is, she had been *born* of the Spirit, but had not been *filled* with the Spirit.

So I said to her, "You don't have the Holy Ghost."

She knew what I meant by that. I knew she had been born of the Spirit and had the witness of the Spirit in her heart that she was a child of God. But she had not been filled with the Holy Spirit with the evidence of speaking in other tongues.

She answered, "No, I don't have the Holy Ghost."

So I just laid my hand on her head again and said, "Receive the Holy Ghost in the Name of Jesus."

Immediately, without stammering or stuttering or waiting a second, she lifted both hands and started talking in tongues instantly.

Later on she said, "If I had known this, I could have had this experience fifteen years ago, and I wouldn't have had to wait until now."

This woman had faith all the time to receive healing, the baptism of the Holy Ghost, or *whatever* she needed from God. She just wasn't *using* her faith.

Don't Take Sides Against God

That's what so many Christians are doing. They're really taking sides against God, against the Bible, and against themselves without recognizing what they're doing.

They wouldn't do it if they knew for sure just what they were doing. But they keep talking about how they don't have any faith. That's taking sides against God, because every time you say you don't have faith, you're unconsciously saying, "God, You lied to me. You told me a lie."

God's Word is *God* speaking! God and His Word are one just like you and your word are one.

You know if your word is no good, you're no good. And if God's Word is no good, then He's no good. But God's Word is good! And God and His Word are one! And God's Word says that you have faith: *"God hath dealt to every man the measure of faith"* (Rom. 12:3).

You have a measure of the God-kind of faith! God's Word says you do. You have a measure of the kind of faith that created the worlds in the beginning. You have a measure of the mountain-moving faith!

One woman said to me, "Yeah, but I know I don't."

"Well," I said, "you or God is lying about it then, because He said you *do* have a measure of the mountain-moving faith."

How in the world can you get God to work *with* you and *for* you with you taking sides against Him? Whether you're taking sides consciously or unconsciously, you're still on the wrong side.

A lot of people are sincere, but they're sincerely wrong. And just because they are sincere doesn't change the fact that they're wrong. So let's just come to the Word and walk in the light of it. God's Word will solve our problems for us.

Let's look again at Ephesians 2:8: *"by grace are ye saved through faith."* So then if a person didn't have faith, he wouldn't be saved, because the Bible says, *"For by grace are ye saved through FAITH; and that not of yourselves: it is the gift of God."*

Notice Paul said that the faith you're saved by is not of yourself; it's not a natural human faith. *God* gave you faith to be saved. That agrees with what he said in Romans 12:3: *"GOD hath dealt to every man the measure of faith."*

But how does God give the sinner faith to be saved? The Bible tells us.

ROMANS 10:17
17 So then faith cometh by hearing, and hearing by the word of God.

If you'll read Romans chapter 10, you'll see that Paul is talking here about salvation and about getting faith to be saved.

ROMANS 10:8

8   But what saith it? The word is nigh thee, even in thy mouth, and in thy heart: that is, the WORD of FAITH, which we preach.

Notice God's Word is called the word of *faith*, because God's Word builds faith. God's Word causes faith to come to the heart of those who are open to it.

ROMANS 10:9–10, 13–14

9   That if thou shalt confess with thy mouth the Lord Jesus, and shalt believe in thine heart that God hath raised him from the dead, thou shalt be saved.

10 For with the heart man believeth unto righteousness; and with the mouth confession is made unto salvation. . . .

13 For whosoever shall call upon the name of the Lord shall be saved.

14 How then shall they call on him in whom they have not believed? and how shall they believe in him of whom they have not HEARD? . . .

You can't believe without hearing, because *"Faith cometh by hearing, and hearing by the word of God"* (Rom. 10:17). That's the way faith comes—by *hearing*! Hearing what? *The Word of God.*

Too many times in services, we hear a little bit of the Word and a whole lot of something else. That's the reason there's not much of a faith-producing element to those services.

I tell folks all the time, "If what you hear preached—whether it's in my meetings or somebody else's meetings—doesn't cause faith to come and build faith in your spirit, then it either isn't the Word of God or else you're not hearing it." The Bible says, *"Faith cometh by hearing, and hearing by the word of God"* (Rom. 10:17).

A lot of times, folks can sit in a meeting, and the Word of God just goes in one ear and out the other ear, so to speak. In other words, they're sitting there in the meeting all right, but they're not listening. But as I said, if what you hear preached doesn't cause faith to come, it either isn't God's Word or else you aren't hearing it.

So many times what we hear preached in many areas and many quarters is really not the Word. Now sometimes folks will quote a scripture and put their own interpretation on it. But that's not going to build faith. Let the scriptures interpret themselves. Find other scriptures beside just one to prove what you're saying. You can't build doctrine on just one verse. The Bible says that in the mouth of two or three witnesses shall every word be established (Deut. 19:15; Matt. 18:16; 2 Cor. 13:1).

I've seen people—even ministers sometimes—take a verse of scripture out of its setting and try to build a doctrine on it. They've done this when, actually, there were other verses of scripture on the same subject they could have used to get a clearer picture of what the Bible was talking about. But they wouldn't listen to the other scriptures, because they wanted it the way *they* believed.

Some fellows seem to have gone to seed on some subjects and have taken them to extremes. And some of those subjects are very unimportant. Sometimes folks have majored in the minors. In other words, instead of majoring in the main subjects in God's Word—the things that are important, like faith—they major in the minor things that aren't as important.

Why Faith Is So Important

Faith is the most important subject in the whole Bible. A preacher asked me one time, "Brother Hagin, you know, I've been preaching for years, and I never preached on the subject of faith yet. Why do you preach on it so much?"

I said, "Because a man who has never preached faith has never preached the Bible. There's not anything in the Bible as important as this subject. You can't even be *saved* without faith, because *'by grace are ye saved through FAITH; and that not of yourselves: it is the gift of God'"* (Eph. 2:8).

I continued: "You can't live for God without faith. You can't please God without faith, because the Bible says, *'Without faith it is impossible to please him'* (Heb. 11:6). The Bible also says, *'we walk by faith, not by sight'* (2 Cor. 5:7).

"This Christian walk is a *faith* walk," I told him. "You can't fight spiritual battles without faith, because the Bible says the only fight we're supposed to fight is the fight of faith. It says, *'Fight the good fight of faith'"* (1 Tim. 6:12).

When I gave that fellow all those scriptures, he just stood there and sort of blinked his eyes.

"Man!" he said. "I'd better get to preaching faith, hadn't I?"

I said, "Yeah, you sure had."

No wonder this preacher and his congregation weren't successful Christians. Instead, they were negative and defeated Christians with the devil holding high carnival in their lives. And it was simply because the real truth had not been preached to them. It's the most difficult thing in the world to receive from God in an atmosphere of doubt—in other words, in an atmosphere that's negative instead of positive.

I remember I was holding a three-week meeting in a certain city several years ago. We had Saturdays off, and on one of the Saturday nights, the pastor said to me, "Brother Hagin, my wife and I are going to drive out to a little suburban town to be in the revival service there tonight. They're having Saturday night services, and we thought maybe you'd like to go with us." I was traveling alone at the time, and so I went with them to the meeting.

It was the third week of this revival meeting. They were going to close out the next night. They made mention to us that they hadn't had a dull service in three weeks, but not one single person had been saved, and not one single person had been baptized in the Holy Ghost.

We'd had about fifty people saved and about fifty-five baptized in the Holy Ghost. People were receiving something from God in our meetings, but they weren't receiving anything in these people's meetings. It didn't take me long before I found out why.

Now don't misunderstand me. They were good people. I simply mean this to be constructive criticism. Destructive criticism is wrong, but I'm not mentioning the name of any person or church, so it doesn't hurt or destroy anybody.

The evangelist got up and preached, and he took a text from the Old Testament. That's perfectly all right if you'll be sure to interpret it in the light of the New Testament. After all, we're not living under the Old Covenant; we're living under the New Covenant. There are some things back there in the Old Testament that really don't apply to us anyhow.

Well, this evangelist happened to get ahold of something back there that really didn't apply to us under the New Covenant at all. And I wondered after he first read it, *What in the world is he going to do with that?*

Here's what he did: He started out by saying, "I've got three points to my sermon," and he proceeded to give point number one. After he'd given his point, he said, "Now let me tell you how I've got this *figured out.*"

The minute he said that, I immediately thought to myself, "Paul told Timothy in Second Timothy 4:2, 'Preach the WORD.' He didn't say, 'Timothy, go tell them how you've got it figured out'!"

I figured out a long time ago that people aren't interested in my opinions. My opinion is no better than yours, and neither one of our opinions is really any good! But what God's Word says *is* important!

After the evangelist said, "Let me tell you how I've got this figured out," he took fifteen minutes to tell how he had it figured out.

I was so disturbed by what this preacher was saying, I didn't know a fellow could sit in church and hurt in so many different places! To tell you the real truth about it, the way he had it "figured out" was ridiculous. It didn't line up with the Word.

Then finally he got to his second point. I was glad he got over the first one, and I hoped he'd get to something a little better. But he got down to his second point and gave it, and then he said, "Now let me give you my *opinion* on this."

Again I thought of what Paul said to Timothy: "Preach the *Word.*" He didn't say, "Timothy, give them your *opinion;* tell them how you've got it *figured out.*"

The evangelist gave us his opinion, and I'll tell you, I struggled through his *opinion!*

He finally announced that he was down to his third point. I sighed a sigh of relief and thought, *Well, maybe he'll give us something now.*

I tell people all the time, "When you go to church, have as much sense as an old cow—eat the hay and leave the sticks!" But so far, in that particular meeting, I hadn't gotten any hay at all—it was all sticks!

I thought maybe this evangelist would give us a little hay. But he presented his third point, and just as soon as he gave it he said, "Now let me give you my *theory* on this."

Oh, brother! This evangelist had said, "Let me tell you how I've got this *figured out,*" "let me give you my *opinion* on this," and "let me give you my *theory* on this." But that's not what God said to do. We are to preach God's *Word!*

You don't have to give your opinion. What you think about something is unimportant. What God says about it, though, is important. In everything, ask yourself, *What does God's Word say?*

After forty-five minutes of that evangelist's discourse, I wasn't surprised that not a soul went forward when he gave an invitation for folks to be saved. I didn't blame them. I wouldn't have gone forward either, because when he gave the invitation, he said, "We're going to give the invitation, and if you're lost—why, come to this altar and pray here. You can't ever tell—God *might* save you."

He actually said that!

I immediately thought about what the Word of God said. Jesus said, *"All that the Father giveth me shall come to me; and him that cometh to me I will in no wise cast out"* (John 6:37). It's not a matter that He *might* save a person. Jesus said, *"I will in no wise cast* [him] *out."*

Stay With the Word

You see, if you give folks the Word, then they'll have faith to come and get saved! But no wonder they didn't come; that evangelist had said, "God *might* save you."

They sang a verse as he gave the altar call, and nobody came. He talked a little bit more and said, "Now come on and pray. It won't hurt you. You can't ever tell, this might be your night."

I immediately thought of what the Scripture says. I would have told people, "This *is* your night. Today is the day of salvation. *Now* is the accepted time" (2 Cor. 6:2).

Nobody came to the altar, so the evangelist said, "I'm not going to keep you. This is Saturday night, and I know we've got to come in the morning to Sunday school and church. But we're going to sing another verse, and if you want to be saved, you just come here to the altar. God might save you. This might be your night."

Then he gave his own experience. Now it's all right to refer to experience if it's in line with the God's Word. But, my friends, experience can be misleading. You can't build on experience. You must build on God's Word and have experiences in line with God's Word.

I'm not interested in experiences as such. In other words, I'm not interested in just having an experience. I'm only interested in having an experience in line with God's Word—in having and experiencing what God's Word says belongs to me!

Many times somebody wants an experience like somebody else's. But God never promised you an experience like somebody else's. He just promised you blessings and benefits according to His Word.

I'm not so sure I'd want somebody else's experience anyhow! I don't doubt that some people have had certain experiences. But if their experiences are not in line with God's Word, I'm not so concerned about them.

For instance, this evangelist gave his experience. He said, "I had to pray three days and three nights before I could get God in the notion of saving me."

When I heard that, I felt the same way you probably feel about it, because it was unscriptural! I immediately thought of what the scripture says about Jesus in the Book of Revelation: *"the Lamb slain from the foundation of the world"* (Rev. 13:8). Jesus is the Lamb slain from the foundation of the world. That means God was in the notion of saving this evangelist before He ever made the world!

That evangelist didn't have to get God in the notion of saving him. God was in the notion of saving him when He sent Jesus! What do you think He sent Jesus for? God so *loved* the world that He *gave*! Isn't that a sign He's in the notion of saving people? Sure it is.

JOHN 3:16

16 For God so loved the world, that he gave his only begotten Son, that whosoever believeth in him should not perish, but have everlasting life.

I would have told people what the Bible says. But this man gave his *opinion* and his *experience*. He said he had to pray three days and three nights before he could get God in the notion of saving him. But he was seeking God and praying in the dark, because he was in unbelief.

I thought to myself, "Dear Lord! Nobody's going to come to the altar. If I were a sinner, I wouldn't come because he just got through telling me I'd probably have to pray three days and nights, and after that I still might not even get saved!"

You see, telling folks what *you* think about something and giving people your opinions and theories only produces unbelief. Paul said, "Preach the *Word*."

Faith comes by hearing the Word! Faith is built on *facts*—on the facts of God's Word. Unbelief is founded on *theories*. That's the reason our churches are so full of unbelief—because they've heard so much theory.

Ministry based on theory thrives on a psychology of unbelief. The poor dear church members are not to blame. They're just a product of what they've heard.

You won't find this definition in the dictionary, but I'll give you my definition of a theory. A "theory" is *a supposition established on ignorance of the subject under discussion!*

You can see from this evangelist that his sermon was all theory. That's because it was established upon ignorance of the subject under discussion! So preach the *Word!*

In helping others, not only as ministers in the pulpit ministry, but as individuals just talking to others, let's tell folks what the Bible says. The best way in the world to help people is to give them what God's Word says, not what some man says. What man says is unimportant. Man can be wrong, but God cannot be wrong. And God cannot fail.

I've proven it over and over again that the most important thing is to give people what God's Word says. I don't care where they are in life or what's happened to them. Find out what God's Word says about the subject and that'll change things.

I remember one time my wife and I were preaching in another state. We had preached many times in that state for a certain Full Gospel denomination. We were in the area again when we heard that the head of the denomination in this particular state went home to be with the Lord. He wasn't really old, but he had put a lot of mileage on his life over the years, and he lived out his life.

Before we left our meeting to go on to another state, my wife and I went by to see the widow of this Full Gospel leader who had passed away. She was greatly overwrought.

Of course, preachers from out of state were coming in along with their wives to visit. All of these people were born-again and Spirit-filled. I get so mad sometimes (I don't know whether it's my righteous indignation or whether I just plain get mad about it) at people playing into the hands of the devil instead of helping people.

For instance, this dear woman was just practically in hysterics when we got there. Everybody who had come along—*Full Gospel preachers*—would say to her about her husband, "What are we going to do without him?"

Well, I know they're going to miss him, but after all, he isn't God. I mean, God's not dead!

But these preachers would get this widow all worked up until she'd almost go into hysterics.

When we got there, I just took her by the hand, led her into the living room, sat her down, opened the Bible, and began to read to her.

I said to her, "Your husband lived his life out and went home. He didn't suffer; he just lay down in bed one night and quit breathing."

This man didn't suffer and go through a lot. It was time for him to go home. It's sort of like the old folks in the Old Testament. God said to Israel, *"I will take sickness away from the midst of thee . . . the number of thy days I will fulfil"* (Exod. 23:25–26).

If you'll read the accounts, you'll find that some of the patriarchs knew when it was time to go, like Jacob, for instance. He laid his hands on his sons and blessed them, and then he gathered his feet up in the bed and gave up the ghost.

So I said to this widow, "Your husband lived out his life, gathered his feet up in bed, and gave up the ghost.

"Now where did he go?" I asked her, and I read from the New Testament where Paul said, *"For to me to live is Christ, and to die is GAIN"* (Phil. 1:21).

I continued: "Of course you feel your loss, but don't be selfish about it." (If you'll notice, nearly all the tears people shed are selfish tears. People think, "Poor old me. What am I going to do?")

I said, "Forget about you. Think about him. I know you feel your loss, but, really, you're not crying about him because you know where he went! He's *gained*!

"For example," I said to her, "you've got a son off in another state. Suppose he writes a letter to you and says, 'I want you to pray for me. The company I work for has just offered me a ten thousand-dollar raise. They're also going to furnish me with a brand-new home with all bills paid.'"

I said, "You wouldn't get up in church and cry and say, 'I want you all to pray for my son. He's been promoted, and, I'll tell you, I don't know whether I can stand it or not.' No, you'd be happy for him for what He's gained. You'd be rejoicing about it."

I said, "Think about your husband—think about what he's gained!"

This woman got to shouting, "Glory to God!" Her face lit up, and the burden rolled away. She dried her tears.

"Yes," she said, "he's gone to Heaven. He's gained all right. That's what the Bible says."

She was just as happy as she could be. In fact, she just started humming a song. She got up and got busy straightening up around the house, and her face was light and bright, just like she was floating around on air.

But then along came some more unbelieving preachers. By the time they stepped up on the porch, they were all hollering and screaming and crying at the top of their voices. "What in the world are we going to do now?" And they got this widow to crying again until she was almost in hysterics.

I had to take her the second time and lead her away from the unbelieving preachers. (I know why Jesus put people out sometimes—because of unbelief!) I sat her back down on the couch in the living room and said, "Now wait just a minute, Sister. You've got your mind back on yourself. Did you notice what these preachers said? They said, 'What are *we* going to do?' See, they're all feeling sorry for *themselves*.

"I'm not being hard about it; I'm just being biblical about it. They're thinking about themselves. Those preachers said, 'What are *we* going to do without him? We'll never make it without him.'"

I said, "Actually, we ought to be dependent on the Lord, not on your husband. I know he was a great man. I preached many months for him. He set up meetings for me in his churches. I appreciated him highly. I feel the loss, but I'm rejoicing in the fact that he's gone home, because to die is gain."

2 CORINTHIANS 5:6–8

6 Therefore we are always confident, knowing that, whilst we are at home in the body, we are absent from the Lord:

7 (For we walk by faith, not by sight:)

8 We are confident, I say, and willing rather to be absent from the body, and to be present with the Lord.

After reading these verses to the woman, I said to her, "Look at the house he lived in—his body. That's not him; he's present with the Lord. He's alive and conscious with all the faculties he ever had. Hallelujah!"

This woman's face lit up, she dried up her tears, and she was happy again. She was like that for a while and then here came some more unbelieving preachers who got her crying again. And I had to take her again and sit her down and go over the Scriptures with her. Then my wife and I had to leave because we had to go on to our meeting. Being in the ministry herself, she understood, so we left.

They had the funeral in another part of the state, and on the very day of the funeral, she called me long distance and said, "Brother Hagin, could I talk to you? You're the only one who helps me. I know other people are concerned, and I realize they all loved my husband. But they don't help me. They pull me down spiritually and sap what little spiritual faith and strength I do have."

She continued: "Just tell me again what you told me before. I know it's all in the Bible." So I took the time to talk to her, praise God, and I'll tell you, she began shouting for joy on the other end of the line!

We went on with our meeting. About the third week we were there, this woman had some business to attend to in the town we were in, and she called us again.

We were going back home to Texas after this meeting. She asked us, "Would it be all right if I come over there and just go home with you?"

We said, "Sure, we'd be glad to have you." She said again, "You're the only ones who really help me and give me something that strengthens me. You put a foundation under me."

I said, "Really, it's not us. It's the Word of God." It's God's Word that strengthens folks and puts a foundation under them.

We read the Word of God together with her and prayed, and her face lit up. And she was happy while she was with us, like she was floating along on a cloud.

We got home to our hometown in Garland, Texas, and for several days, this woman was doing just fine. She went shopping with my wife, and she was happy. Her husband had died just a month earlier, but she was doing good. She wasn't happy because her husband had died. Certainly, she still felt her loss, but she was glad because her husband had lived his full length of time out, and he'd worked for God for many years.

One day she said, "Well, I ought to call _____" (and she mentioned the name of a couple who used to work under her husband). They were pastoring a church in Dallas, so she called them. They wanted to come out and visit.

I knew what would happen, so I stayed close by. And sure enough, by the time they got out of the car, both the man and wife—*preachers*—were crying at the top of their voices. I know our neighbors must have thought some of *us* had died!

Of course, she went out to meet this couple, and they said, "What in the world are you going to do? How will you ever make it without him?"

And they got her in tears again. I kept quiet for a little while, and then finally I butted in (and I'm pretty good about doing that!). I said, "You know, I think we really ought to depend upon the Lord, because He is our Helper, and He is our Strengthener." I turned the conversation in a different direction, because I could see this woman was getting worked up almost into hysterics.

Finally, her visitors left. She said to my wife and me, "You know, I don't believe I'll call anybody else. There's some other preachers here who used to work with my husband, whom he helped get started in the ministry. But they've all got a sad tale. I know they'll work on my emotions and get me all worked up, and I shouldn't allow myself to get that way. After all, I know where he went.

"If it's all right with you, I'll just stay here for a while longer, because you help me."

Well, God's Word will do that for folks! No matter what the circumstance of life, God's Word has something to say about it. And that's really the only way you're ever going to help anybody or put anything into them that will really benefit them. It's not by giving them your opinion, but by telling them what God's Word says about it.

So many times in dealing with people who are going through tests, trials, and temptations, we just try to help them naturally. "Don't worry about it," some folks say. "It'll all come out in the wash."

But that's not what the Bible says. Let people know that right in the midst of the test and trial, the Lord said, "I'll never leave you nor forsake you" (Heb. 13:5). He's there, praise God! Let people know that the Bible says, *"Greater is he that is in you, than he that is in the world"* (1 John 4:4). That's what the Word says. And that will put faith and confidence into them.

1 JOHN 4:4
4 Ye are of God, little children, and have overcome them: because greater is he that is in you, than he that is in the world.

Very often I ask people, "What's the Holy Ghost doing in you? Is He just a spiritual hitchhiker, hitchhiking a ride with you through life? No! He's in you to help you—to strengthen and comfort you. Smith Wigglesworth said, "I'm a thousand times bigger on the inside than I am on the outside." Hallelujah!

So put God's Word into people. That's the best way in the world to help them.

I'll give you one more verse of scripture that will be the clincher that proves that every believer has a measure of the God-kind of faith.

We already read Romans 12:3, Ephesians 2:8, and Romans 10:17. Mark all of these verses in your Bible. The Bible said, *"In the mouth of two or three witnesses every word may be established"* (Matt. 18:16). I already gave you three witnesses, so I'll give you *four* witnesses altogether. I've been driving the nail in the board with the other scriptures. Now I'm going to clinch it on the other side of the board with this scripture!

2 CORINTHIANS 4:13

13 We HAVING the same spirit of faith, according as it is written, I believed, and therefore have I spoken; we also believe, and therefore speak.

The Apostle Paul is doing the writing. He's writing to the Church at Corinth, and he includes himself with the Church at Corinth. What applies to the Church at Corinth applies to the Church in your hometown today. It applies to the Church anywhere. So we know who Paul is writing to in this verse. He is writing to believers.

He says, *"We HAVING the same spirit of faith."* Paul says *"having,"* not *trying to get,* not *praying for it,* not *hoping for it,* not *struggling to get it.* We *have* it.

What spirit of faith is it that we have? *"According as it is written, I believed, and therefore have I spoken; we also believe, and therefore speak"* (2 Cor. 4:13).

That's the same spirit of faith or the same kind of faith that Jesus is talking about in Mark 11:22–24, especially in verse 23.

MARK 11:23

23 For verily I say unto you, That whosoever shall say unto this mountain, Be thou removed, and be thou cast into the sea; and SHALL NOT DOUBT IN HIS HEART, but SHALL BELIEVE that those things which he SAITH shall come to pass; he shall have whatsoever he saith.

2 CORINTHIANS 4:13

13 We having the same spirit of faith, according as it is written, I BELIEVED, and therefore have I SPOKEN; we also BELIEVE, and therefore SPEAK.

Isn't this verse talking about the same spirit of faith? Sure it is. And Paul said we *have* it. *Every* believer has it."

The faith that Mark 11:23 and Second Corinthians 4:13 talks about is the God-kind of faith, and every believer already has a measure of this God-kind of faith.

I want you to concentrate on this truth, because it's scriptural—it's in the Bible. And I want you to say out loud: "I'm a believer. I'm not a doubter. I have a measure of the God-kind of faith. I have a measure of the kind of faith that created the worlds in the beginning. I have a measure of the mountain-moving faith."

Listen to yourself say that over and over again until it registers on your spirit. Once God's Word gets down there in your spirit, into your heart, it will control your life.

Chapter Two

Ever-Increasing Faith

We read in chapter 1 that every believer has a measure of the God-kind of faith—a measure of the faith that created the worlds in the beginning. *Every believer* has a measure of the mountain-moving faith!

ROMANS 12:3
3 . . . according as God hath dealt to every man the measure of faith.

EPHESIANS 2:8
8 For by grace are ye saved through faith; and that not of yourselves: it is the gift of God.

ROMANS 10:17
17 So then faith cometh by hearing, and hearing by the word of God.

The clincher is Second Corinthians 4:13.

2 CORINTHIANS 4:13
13 We HAVING the same spirit of faith, according as it is written, I BELIEVED, and therefore have I SPOKEN; we also BELIEVE, and therefore SPEAK.

Notice we're not trying to get faith. We're not praying for it. We *have* it.

From this verse, you can readily see that this is the same spirit of faith that Jesus talked about in Mark 11:23, because He said, *"Whosoever shall say unto this mountain, Be thou removed, and be thou cast unto the sea; and shall not doubt in his heart, but shall*

BELIEVE that those things which he SAITH shall come to pass; he shall have whatsoever he saith."

Every believer already has a measure of the God-kind of faith. You see, God gets everybody started off the same way. He doesn't give one more faith than He does another one. He gives to every man the measure of faith (Rom. 12:3). Then your faith grows according to what you do with it.

A lot of people have done with their faith what the fellow in the Bible did with his one talent (Matt. 25:25). They've just wrapped their faith up in a napkin and hid it. They haven't used it.

It's up to you what you do with the measure of faith God has given you. So my second thought to you is this: *This measure of faith can be increased.* But you're the one who increases it, not God.

Certainly God furnishes the means whereby faith can be increased. But this measure of faith is increased by doing two things: *feeding it on the Word of God* and *exercising it or putting it into practice.*

The Bible very often uses natural, human terms to teach spiritual thoughts. For example, this is how Jesus taught in Matthew 4:4.

MATTHEW 4:4
4 . . . Man shall not live by bread alone, but by every word that proceedeth out of the mouth of God.

Jesus is using a natural, human idea to convey a spiritual thought. He's saying to us that what bread or food is to the body, the Word of God is to the spirit—to the heart of man.

You know that if you eat good food regularly, it will build you up physically. But even if you eat right but don't exercise, all you'll do is get flabby and out of shape.

In much the same way, you need to feed your faith on God's Word. But you also need to *exercise* your faith, because if you don't, your faith muscles will be flabby. They won't be able to do much spiritually in the way of moving mountains in your life.

I've seen people who were big people, yet they could hardly lift any weight at all. They hadn't used their muscles. Then I've seen some little fellow come along and lift weights over his head that a big fellow couldn't even get off the ground!

What made the difference? Was it size? No, because the one fellow was bigger than the other fellow. But he hadn't *used* his muscles. That's what made the difference. The big fellow fed his body, but he hadn't exercised it.

You can feed your spirit and feed your faith, because God's Word is faith food. But you also need to exercise your faith in order to develop it and cause it to grow.

ROMANS 10:8

8 But what saith it? The word is nigh thee, even in thy mouth, and in thy heart: that is, the word of faith, which we preach.

Paul called the message he preached the *word of faith*. He calls the Word of God the *word of faith*, because the Word will cause faith to come into your heart (Rom. 10:17). God's Word will build assurance, confidence, and faith in your spirit or heart. Then you're to exercise that faith.

So we know that the measure of faith we've received can be increased by doing two things: by feeding it on God's Word and putting it into practice or exercising it in everyday living.

Faith Is Measurable

One person said, "You either have faith or you don't have it." In other words, this person was trying to say that you couldn't have more or less faith.

But that's not true. You have more or less faith. Remember, it's up to you what you do with the measure of faith God has given you. For example, your faith can grow. Second Thessalonians 1:3 says, *"we are bound to thank God always for you, brethren, as it is meet, because that your FAITH GROWETH EXCEEDINGLY."*

So God is saying faith can grow. Well, since faith can grow, then it can be great or small or more or less. Let's look at several other statements Jesus made about faith.

LUKE 12:28
28 If then God so clothe the grass, which is today in the field, and tomorrow is cast into the oven; how much more will he clothe you, O YE OF LITTLE FAITH?

MATTHEW 6:30
30 Wherefore, if God so clothe the grass of the field, which to day is, and to morrow is cast into the oven, shall he not much more clothe you, O YE OF LITTLE FAITH?

MATTHEW 14:22–31
22 And straightway Jesus constrained his disciples to get into a ship, and to go before him unto the other side, while he sent the multitudes away.

23 And when he had sent the multitudes away, he went up into a mountain apart to pray: and when the evening was come, he was there alone.

24 But the ship was now in the midst of the sea, tossed with waves: for the wind was contrary.

25 And in the fourth watch of the night Jesus went unto them, walking on the sea.

26 And when the disciples saw him walking on the sea, they were troubled, saying, It is a spirit; and they cried out for fear.

27 But straightway Jesus spake unto them, saying, Be of good cheer; it is I; be not afraid.

28 And Peter answered him and said, Lord, if it be thou, bid me come unto thee on the water.

29 And he said, Come. And when Peter was come down out of the ship, he walked on the water, to go to Jesus.

30 But when he saw the wind boisterous, he was afraid; and beginning to sink, he cried, saying, Lord, save me.

31 And immediately Jesus stretched forth his hand, and caught him, and said unto him, O THOU OF LITTLE FAITH, wherefore didst thou doubt?

In these verses, Jesus is speaking about little faith. He said to Peter, *"O thou of LITTLE FAITH, wherefore didst thou doubt."*

In Matthew chapter 8, Jesus commended the faith of the centurion who came to Him on the behalf of his servant. Jesus said the centurion had *great* faith.

MATTHEW 8:5–10, 13

5 And when Jesus was entered into Capernaum, there came unto him a centurion, beseeching him,

6 And saying, Lord, my servant lieth at home sick of the palsy, grievously tormented.

7 And Jesus saith unto him, I will come and heal him.

8 The centurion answered and said, Lord, I am not worthy that thou shouldest come under my roof: but speak the word only, and my servant shall be healed.

9 For I am a man under authority, having soldiers under me: and I say to this man, Go, and he goeth; and to another, Come, and he cometh; and to my servant, Do this, and he doeth it.

10 When Jesus heard it, he marvelled, and said to them that followed, Verily I say unto you, I have not found so GREAT FAITH, no, not in Israel. . . .

13 And Jesus said unto the centurion, Go thy way; and as thou hast believed, so be it done unto thee. And his servant was healed in the selfsame hour.

Jesus said to the disciples about the centurion, *"I have not found so great faith, no, not in Israel"* (v. 10). So in these verses Jesus speaks to one man that he had *great* faith and to another man that he had *little* faith.

We can see from these verses that a person's faith can be little or great. Jesus said it could. Now notice that in Romans 4:19, the Word of God speaks of *weak* faith.

ROMANS 4:19
19 And being not WEAK IN FAITH, he considered not his own body now dead, when he was about an hundred years old, neither yet the deadness of Sarah's womb.

The very next verse speaks of *strong* faith.

ROMANS 4:20
20 He staggered not at the promise of God through unbelief; but was STRONG IN FAITH, giving glory to God.

From these verses, we can conclude that since faith can be weak or strong, or if faith can be little or great, then it can be less or more.

Faith is *measurable*.

We already mentioned that the Bible talks about *growing* faith (2 Thess. 1:3). Then James 2:5 mentions *rich* faith.

JAMES 2:5
5 Harken, my beloved brethren, Hath not God chosen the poor of this world RICH IN FAITH, and heirs of the kingdom which he hath promised to them that love him?

Acts 6:5 says Stephen was *full of faith.*

ACTS 6:5
5 And the saying pleased the whole multitude: and they chose Stephen, a man FULL OF FAITH and of the Holy Ghost. . . .

Well, if you could be *full* of faith, you could be *half-full* of faith too. If a glass is *full* of water, by the same token, it can be half-full of water, or even a third-full of water.

James 2:22 speaks of a *perfect* faith.

JAMES 2:22
22 Seest thou how faith wrought with his works, and by works was FAITH MADE PERFECT?

First Timothy 1:5 speaks of *unfeigned* faith or faith that is genuine and sincere.

1 TIMOTHY 1:5
5 Now the end of the commandment is charity out of a pure heart, and of a good conscience, and of FAITH UNFEIGNED.

First Timothy 1:19 speaks of *shipwrecked faith.*

1 TIMOTHY 1:19
19 Holding faith, and a good conscience; which some having put away CONCERNING FAITH HAVE MADE SHIPWRECK.

Also, First John 5:4 speaks of *overcoming* faith.

1 JOHN 5:4
4   For whatsoever is born of God overcometh the world: and this is the victory
    that OVERCOMETH THE WORLD, EVEN OUR FAITH.

As I said before, the Bible says, "In the mouth of two or three
witnesses shall every word be established" (Matt. 18:16). But I gave
you more than ten witnesses! And all of these verses will prove to you
that *faith is measurable.*

Your Faith Should Constantly Be Growing

We know that the measure of faith every believer has can be
increased. *Your measure of faith can be increased by feeding it on the
Word of God and by exercising it or by putting it into practice.*

George Mueller, founder of an orphanage in Bristol, England,
years ago, was a man of faith. The orphanage he founded was just
strictly a faith project. He didn't have any church because he wasn't
pastoring, so he couldn't take up any offerings to help support these
orphan children.

Eventually, Rev. Mueller wound up with as many as 2,500 orphans
in his home for children. He was solely responsible to believe God for
the food and clothing to feed and clothe 2,500 children! Also, he had
to believe God for the money to build the buildings to house 2,500
children, plus the money to pay the attendants' salaries and for the
upkeep of the orphanage property.

Rev. Mueller didn't have a mailing list to let people know what he
was doing so he could ask for their help. And there were no radios in

those days. He had no way to publish information about his orphanage in order to solicit prayers and financial support.

Of course, the news about what he was doing would get out by word of mouth. But Rev. Mueller simply had to believe God for the money to run his orphanage. And in his lifetime, he prayed in $7,500,000. That doesn't sound too big in these days of inflation, but that was a lot of money in those days. That would probably be like $30 or $35 million today.

When he was 93 years old, Mueller wrote these words in his journal: "When I first started praying and believing God [in other words, exercising or using his measure of faith], it took all the faith I had to believe God for one American dollar. But after feeding and exercising my faith daily for fifty years, I could believe God for one million dollars just as easily as I could for only one dollar fifty years before."

Rev. Mueller said, "I always begin the day by feeding on God's Word, not just reading it." Before he ever ate breakfast—before he ever fed his body—he fed his spirit man on God's Word.

Smith Wigglesworth, another English preacher, was also a man of great faith. He always carried his Bible or his New Testament with him. He said, "I never considered myself thoroughly dressed unless I had my Bible or my Testament in my pocket." He would have just as soon gone out without his shoes on as to be without his Bible.

As a traveling minister in his day, Wigglesworth stayed in a lot of people's homes as he traveled all over the world. And many people have said that after every meal, even if he was in a restaurant or a cafe, Wigglesworth would always push back from the table, get out his Testament and say, "Well, we've fed the body; now let's feed the inward man." And he'd start reading, and he'd read something about faith and usually wind up giving a little faith message.

F. F. Bosworth said, "Most Christians feed their bodies three hot meals a day, and their spirit one cold snack a week. And they wonder why they're so weak in faith."

Well, if you just ate one cold snack a week physically, you'd grow *weak* physically! The same is true spiritually. God's Word is faith food!

You see, a lot of times people are praying, "Oh God, give me faith," but they're paying no attention at all to the means He's put in their hands to produce faith—the Bible.

Well, God can't answer that prayer, because in a sense, He's already answered it. He's already told you in His Word how faith comes: *"By hearing, and hearing by the word of God"* (Rom. 10:17).

Many folks think if they could just find out how faith comes, they'd have it made. Well, how does faith come? By hearing. Does it come by praying? No! It comes by *hearing* the Word of God.

God demands faith of us as believers. The Bible says He does.

HEBREWS 11:6

6 But WITHOUT FAITH IT IS IMPOSSIBLE to please him: for he that cometh to God must believe that he is, and that he is a rewarder of them that diligently seek him.

If God demanded that we have faith when it's impossible for us to have faith, we'd have a right to challenge His justice. But if He places in our hands the means whereby faith can be produced, then the responsibility is ours whether or not we have faith.

We read that George Mueller at 93 years of age could exercise his faith and believe God for one million dollars after 50 years as easily as he could for one dollar earlier in his ministry.

Mueller had what Smith Wigglesworth called "an ever-increasing faith"! He had what the Apostle Paul called "exceedingly growing faith" (2 Thess. 1:3). In other words, he started out with the same measure of faith every believer starts out with. But his faith grew and moved mountains!

Start Where You Are

The trouble with a lot of folks is they want to start out at the million-dollar mark. And because that doesn't work for them, they give up on faith.

No, you've got to start out where you are. Nobody climbs a ladder starting on the top rung. You've got to start on the bottom rung and climb up if you're going to climb the ladder. That's the thing that defeats a lot of people—they try to believe beyond their measure of faith.

Just because someone has fed more on God's Word and has exercised their faith is not a sign that God gave them more faith than He gave someone else. No, the person who fed on the Word and exercised his faith had the same measure of faith to begin with as others had. But he fed his faith and exercised it, and his faith grew. Then he could believe God for more.

Somebody said, "I believe I'll start right where Mueller was in his faith." Well, *Mueller* didn't even start there! He got there at ninety-three years of age. He started back on the bottom rung. He started on the one-dollar rung and kept climbing until he got to the one-million-dollar mark!

I can remember in my own life, at one time it took all the faith I had to believe God for $150 a week! That's the truth! I mean I pared everything off my budget that I could, right down to a bare minimum. And it took all the faith I had to believe God for $150.

But after feeding and *using* my faith through the years, I could believe God today for one million dollars for the work of the ministry just as easy as I could believe for $150 forty years ago.

In fact, I believe it was really a little easier for me on the one million than it was on the $150. But forty years ago, if I'd tried to believe God for that much money, I would have fallen flat on my face, because my faith wasn't up there.

That's the thing that defeats a lot of people. They'll hear faith taught, and they'll try to start on the top rung of the ladder or about halfway up the ladder when they're not up there yet. And then it doesn't work for them. Well, naturally it won't work. Faith has to be fed and developed in order for it to grow. And that takes time.

So just begin where you are. Feed and exercise your faith where you are, and it will grow. Then you can believe God for more and more. And after a while, you'll believe God for things you never thought you could—things beyond even your wildest imagination today. And it'll be just as easy to believe God for those things as it is to believe for something little today. Your faith can grow and move mountains!

I think very often we make a mistake trying to push people to believe beyond their faith. We shouldn't criticize people because they don't believe for as much as know belongs to them in Christ. But we certainly have to preach faith to folks so they can get started.

I remember the last church I pastored. There was a woman in our church who was facing major surgery. I knew, of course, that God's best for her and His perfect will for her was that she be healed by the power of God and not have to undergo the surgery.

So I kept talking to her about healing, and I read God's Word to her, trying to raise her level of faith to where mine was and to where God wanted her to be. But I saw over a period of time that I just wasn't making any headway.

Find Something You Can Agree On

So one day I said to her, "Now I've done my best to get you to agree with me. You know the Bible says, 'If two of you on earth shall agree as touching anything they ask, it shall be done' (Matt. 18:19). However, that also means if they don't agree, it won't be done."

You see, you're not going to get somebody healed when you believe they receive their healing, and they believe they receive it. There's no agreement there!

A lot of times people have thought, "If somebody else has enough faith, he can believe God, and I'll just get healed whether I believe or whether I don't."

Well, then, why didn't Jesus go ahead and get everyone healed on His own faith in Nazareth!

MARK 6:5
5   And he could there do no mighty work, save that he laid his hands upon a few sick folk, and healed them.

How come Jesus only got a few sick folk healed in Nazareth? Why didn't He just go ahead and believe God for all of them? Wasn't He a man of faith? Certainly He was. Let's read the next verse.

MARK 6:6
6   And he marvelled BECAUSE OF THEIR UNBELIEF. . . .

If Jesus' faith couldn't override those people's unbelief, you needn't think you're going to do something Jesus couldn't do! You won't be able to get everyone healed on your faith either!

So I endeavored to get this woman to the place of faith where she could receive her healing. But I saw I just wasn't making it. So I said to her, "Sister, I've tried to get you to come up on my level of faith where we could agree together, and I see I'm just not making it. I'll tell you what I'll do. I'll just come down on *your* level of faith.

"Now, then, what can you believe?" I asked her. "I'll just believe with you where you can believe."

"Well," the woman responded, "I can believe that God will see me safely through this operation."

According to Your Faith Be It Unto You

Now don't misunderstand me. That wasn't God's best for this woman. But right on the other hand, if you need to be operated on, if you'll believe that God will see you safely through an operation, the Bible says, *"ACCORDING TO YOUR FAITH be it unto you."* (Matt. 9:29).

It's not that this woman just couldn't believe for her healing. She was a believer, so she could have believed. But she wouldn't and didn't believe she could receive the healing that actually belonged to her in Christ. She didn't believe she would not need to have the operation.

I said to this woman, "I'll just agree with you then that God will see you safely through the operation." So I laid my hand on her head and said to her, "Now you listen to me pray, and see if you can agree with this prayer. And if we agree, it'll be done."

And so I prayed: "Heavenly Father, I know You provided healing for us—for this sister—but she has not yet come to that level of faith to accept it. So I'll come down on her level of faith. You're not going to forsake her, Lord. She's Your child. I'll agree with her that You'll just guide the physician's hands and that You'll bring her safely through this operation. I agree that You'll cause her to respond so quickly, beyond what nature could do, so that even the doctors themselves will admit it's a miracle. In Jesus' Name, amen."

Then I said, "Do you agree with that?"

"Yes," she said, "I agree with that."

I said, "All right, we've found something we can agree on then."

I think Christians ought to agree like that more often. We ought to find things we can *agree* on, instead of finding things we *disagree* on! (And if we do disagree, we ought to be able to disagree without being disagreeable.)

Also, we ought to help people regardless of where they are in their faith walk. This woman couldn't agree on my level of faith, so I came down and agreed on *her* level of faith.

So the woman had the operation. I was at the hospital when she was operated on. They put her to sleep at about 7:30 in the morning and performed the operation.

One of the doctors said to me, "We made a little longer incision than we would ordinarily make, because we wanted to do a little more exploratory surgery while we were performing the operation."

By noon, she was out from under the anesthesia, and she was fully conscious. That night at about eight o'clock, my wife and I were visiting the woman again when the doctor came in. A nurse was with him, and he had this woman's medical chart in his hands. He hadn't seen the woman since her operation early that morning. He said to her, "I see on the chart that you haven't had any medication for pain. Aren't you hurting?"

"No," she answered.

"Have you got *any* pain?" the doctor asked her.

"No."

"Aw," he said, "I know you're bound to be hurting after having your stomach cut wide open."

"Well," she said, "I don't. I don't have one pain; I don't hurt at all."

"Well," he said, "I'm going to mark on your chart for them to give you a shot anyway." They gave her one shot, and that's all they ever gave her. She never had another shot for pain.

About two or three days later, that same doctor said to me, "I've never seen anything like that in my life. We operate on people who come here from all over the United States. We perform three to ten of these operations every single day, and we've done that for years.

"If some other doctor had told me that this woman experienced no pain after this kind of operation, I wouldn't have believed it. If I hadn't seen it myself with my own eyes, I wouldn't have believed it. I've never seen anybody in my lifetime come through this kind of operation so quickly and do so well. It's nothing short of miraculous."

We got what we believed for! It really wasn't the best that God had for this woman. But that was the measure she had grown to, so I just agreed with her. And what we agreed on *happened*!

Be Faithful to Develop Your Faith Life

Afterward, I saw that same woman begin to develop in faith after she had used her faith down on that lower level. And I saw her develop in faith until her faith grew to the point that if she ever faced the same kind of major surgery again, she would have been able to receive her healing instead. She wouldn't have had the operation.

Actually, I would say she developed her faith until she outstripped everyone else in the church in the area of faith. Her faith was developed beyond all of them. Now just a couple of years before, it wasn't. But she started using her faith.

I got this woman to begin using her faith where she was, and she saw that God worked a miracle in her life in that operation. It wasn't His best for her, but, after all, it was a miracle. She never did need a shot for pain after being cut wide open. She didn't even need the one they gave her! And that's what we agreed on—that she would come out of the operation miraculously.

So she began to see that faith *does* work. And she began to use her faith in other areas until within a two-year period, she developed in faith beyond any other member of the church. She developed her measure of the mountain-moving faith.

But this woman could have taken the wrong attitude. She could have said, "Well, I couldn't believe God for healing. I tried it and it didn't work." And she could have just given up on the whole thing and never grown anymore spiritually. She would have still been a spiritual dwarf, or a spiritual baby, not able to help herself or anybody else.

It makes all the difference in the world the attitude we take wherever we are in life. So keep a positive attitude, and keep the switch of faith turned on, praise God! Keep believing God and exercising your faith where you are in your faith walk. Your measure of faith can grow and move mountains!

Chapter Three

Real Faith Is of the Heart

For verily I say unto you, That whosoever shall say unto this mountain, Be thou removed, and be thou cast into the sea; and shall not doubt IN HIS HEART, but shall believe that those things which he saith shall come to pass; he shall have whatsoever he saith.

—Mark 11:23

We read in chapters 1 and 2 two important facts about faith: Every believer has a measure of the mountain-moving faith. And every believer's measure of faith can grow.

The third most important thing about faith is that *faith is of the heart, not the head.* Notice the expression in Mark 11:23, *"and shall NOT DOUBT IN HIS HEART, but shall BELIEVE."* This is talking about believing in your *heart.*

ROMANS 10:10
10 For with the HEART man believeth unto righteousness; and with the mouth confession is made unto salvation.

Faith—that is, Bible faith, or scriptural faith—is of the heart. The real faith is heart-faith, not head-faith.

Well, just what is the heart of man and what does it mean to believe with the heart? The best way in the world to answer that question is to just let the Bible tell you. That will settle all arguments.

First of all, the heart of man, or the human spirit, is not the physical heart that pumps blood throughout your body and keeps you alive. That's not what God is talking about when He talks about the heart of man.

No, let's let God tell us what the heart of man is.

1 PETER 3:4
4 But let it be the hidden MAN OF THE HEART, in that which is not corruptible, even the ornament of a meek and quiet spirit, which is in the sight of God of great price.

Then notice it says that this man of the heart is a *hidden* man. That is, he's hidden to the physical senses. You can't see him with your physical eye or feel him with your physical hand, because he's not a physical being. The inward man—the hidden man of the heart—is a spirit man.

Paul made mention of this inward man in Second Corinthians 4:16.

2 CORINTHIANS 4:16
16 For which cause we faint not; but though our outward man perish [decays], yet the inward man is renewed day by day.

Paul said there's an outward man and an inward man. The outward man is the body. You can see the outward man. And the outward man is decaying; it's growing older.

I realize that people of great faith can be physically younger-looking as they get older. But sometimes people can be so foolish. The Bible plainly says right here in Second Corinthians 4:16 that the outward man is decaying; it's growing older. That's the reason you get wrinkles in your face after a while. You usually get more grey-headed or white-headed as you get older. And your body just doesn't have the reflexes of a young person.

I realize that some folks are further along in faith than others, and very often some people, because of their faith, are physically younger-looking as they get older. And I believe if we're taught correctly and realize that the life of God is in us, that life can be manifested in our mortal flesh even now, and we could live a little longer than a lot of folks.

However, God didn't tell us that we're going to live in the flesh forever. Certainly not! Yet there are people who believe they will never die physically. I met one of these people once. He said, "I don't understand all that talk about dying, going to Heaven, and seeing Jesus and your loved ones who've departed and gone on to Heaven."

"Well, what don't you understand about it?" I asked him. "It's all in the Bible."

"Yes," he answered, "but Jesus said that whoever believes in Him shall never die."

"Oh," I said, "I always wondered what that meant." (I knew what it meant, but I was trying to prove a point to this gentleman.)

I continued: "The Lord said to Martha after her brother, Lazarus, had died, *'Whosoever liveth and believeth in me shall never die. Believest thou this?'"* (John 11:26).

I said, "I always wondered what that meant. Let's see, that must mean that if I'm alive physically here in this earth, and I believe on Jesus, I'll never die physically."

"Yes, that's right! That's right!" the man answered.

"All right," I said, "then maybe you can help me with *this* verse," and I quoted First John 3:14.

1 JOHN 3:14
14 We know that we have passed from death unto life, because we love the brethren. . . .

I asked, "Does this verse mean that we pass from physical death to physical life and that we won't ever die physically?"

"That's right."

"Well, now," I said, "maybe you can help me with *this* verse.

"In Philippians 1:21, the Apostle Paul said, *'For to me to live is Christ, and to die is gain.'* He's saying that physical death is gain!

"Also, notice what Paul said in verse 24: *'Nevertheless to abide in the flesh is more needful for you.'*"

You see, for Paul to live in the flesh was more needful for the Church at Philippi because he could teach them and minister to them.

PHILIPPIANS 1:23–24
23 For I am in a strait betwixt two, having a desire to depart, and to be with Christ; which is far better:
24 Nevertheless to abide in the flesh is more needful for you.

When I quoted those verses, the man said, "Oh, I never have been able to figure out what Paul meant by that!"

"You don't have to figure it out," I answered. "He meant just what he said."

Then the man said to me, "But, you know, Paul didn't make it."

"Oh," I said, "he didn't?"

"No. He didn't make it; he died."

"Well," I said, "if Paul didn't make it, you might as well forget it right now, because you'll never make it either. But even if Paul didn't make it, because he died, it looks like some of those Early Church members would have made it. And if just one of them could have lived forever in the flesh, he'd still be here now. But none of them are here."

That fellow moved out of town shortly after that, and months later he wrote me a letter. When I opened it, there was an offering in it. He said to me, "Brother Hagin, I want you to know that I've gotten born-again and baptized in the Holy Ghost.

"I went one Sunday night to a Full Gospel church and got saved. The pastor may think it was the sermon he preached that caused me to give my heart to God. But I don't know one word he said. I just went to that church because it was like the one you pastor. I knew they believed like you do. It wasn't his sermon at all that caused me to give my heart to God. It was what you said to me."

He continued: "I couldn't get away from the thought that if Paul never made it, I might as well forget thinking I could make it.

"I got to thinking about what you said. Paul was an apostle, a man of God who wrote about half of the New Testament. But like you once said, why in the world would we want to follow a man who never made it?

"I saw how ridiculous that sounded, and I knew I must be wrong. I'd been mistaught. I realized it was like you said—those verses were talking about *spiritual* death, not *physical* death. But I'd taken the scriptures that apply to spiritual death and applied them to physical death."

He added: "Now I know I've passed from death unto life and that I'm spiritually alive unto God. And I'm looking forward to the day when I will have a new, glorified body."

At the bottom of his letter, he said, "Brother Hagin, I want to thank you again. I'm enclosing this offering to help you. I'm not trying to pay you anything; I know I could never do that. But I'm sending you this money just to show you my appreciation and to help you get the truth over to somebody else."

He also said, "For years, I've argued with preachers and other people on this subject. But you never argued with me at all. You just gave me the scripture. I appreciate the fact in that you took time with me. A lot of folks wouldn't even talk to me. They'd just turn around and walk off and leave me. But you showed loved toward me."

Well, I didn't love his wrong thinking. God didn't love all that wrongness about him, but God loved *him*. You see, God doesn't love sin, but He loves the sinner.

In fact, the Bible says that God hates sin. But He doesn't hate the sinner. He loves the sinner. So I showed love toward this man, and he couldn't get away from what I said to him. I was kind to him, and it brought forth fruit in the process of time.

That man just found out that the Bible means what it says. The outward man *is* decaying—the Bible says so. Some people do retain their youth more than others. But the outward man is still decaying. It's the inward man that is renewed day by day (2 Cor. 4:16).

I remember in my home town of McKinney, Texas, there was a fellow by the name of Brother Smith. His church believed in a second definite work of grace and sanctification after the new birth.

Their thinking was that it's all right whether or not you speak with tongues. But he was strong in the area of divine healing, because he had been well taught on the subject. He is an example of someone who retained his youth to a great extent, even when he was up in age.

Many years ago I scheduled some meetings to come back to my hometown of McKinney to preach two or three nights in my home church. It was a Full Gospel church.

Brother Smith came out to one of my meetings even though he wasn't a member of that church.

When the service was over, he said to me, "You know, Brother Hagin, I always liked to hear you preach because you always preach positive—you always preach on faith and healing. I like that."

He continued: "Brother Hagin, I'll be 90 years old in three weeks. And you know, I'm just as good a man—just as strong—in every way as I was as a young man." And he looked good.

He said, "God's kept me. You know, I haven't been sick in 40 years. I got to reading in the Bible one day where Jesus said, 'The very hairs of your head are numbered' (Matt. 10:30; Luke 12:7). In other words, He knows just how many hairs you have in your head.

"I got to thinking about that years ago. And I said to the Lord, 'Well, Lord, You know how many hairs I have. I'm just going to believe You to keep my hair.'" So at age 90, this man had all of his hair.

Not only that, but Brother Smith at 90 years of age had only a few grey hairs. He believed God to keep his hair from turning grey.

My wife had never met Brother Smith before that night. Later I asked her, "If Brother Smith hadn't told us, how old would you think he is?" She said, "Not a day over 55."

Brother Smith was also a man of wealth, yet he'd get out and work every day. In fact, he'd outwork most young men.

After Brother Smith shook hands with us, he started to go. But then he came back and said, "Brother Kenneth, I'll tell you something else. I also believed God to keep my teeth." And he opened his mouth and showed me he had every tooth in his head, and there was not a filling in one of them. They were all his own teeth at 90 years of age!

I'd never thought of that! I'd had one or two fillings, but after that, I never had any more!

Now you understand that this is beyond just divine healing. But right on the other hand, the Bible says, "According to your faith be it unto you" (Matt. 9:29). Brother Smith believed God would do it according to His Word, and God did it.

Brother Smith started to walk away the third time, and then he came back. He said, "Brother Kenneth, I'll tell you the secret of the whole thing. You already know it, but I'll tell you anyway." He said, "I asked God first of all to help me keep *this*—to help me keep my tongue," and he stuck his tongue out.

That is what I want you to see, and it has everything in the world to do with a person living a long life and staying healthy.

You see, the Bible says, *"he that will love life, and see good days, let him refrain his tongue from evil, and his lips that they speak no guile"* (1 Peter 3:10).

When he said that, I remembered an incident that happened years before when I used to work for Brother Smith.

There was a fellow in our hometown who was a World War I veteran. He'd been gassed in the war, and if you know anything about what happened to some of those fellows, you know the after-effects were devastating. They would have spells from time to time, and they were affected mentally.

After this fellow had gotten out of the war, he stayed in the hospital a lot. And when he got out, he took to drinking.

He wasn't a Christian man, of course. If he'd been a Christian, he wouldn't have done some of the terrible things he did. But he began drinking, trying to escape from his physical condition because he'd been gassed in the war. And when he'd get drunk, he'd get mean. He'd just run people off the sidewalk and cut them with a knife. He cut two or three people up pretty severely, and they had to be put in the hospital.

McKinney was a small town of about eight or nine thousand people. And in McKinney, there wasn't anybody who could handle this drunk fellow except Ed Blakeman, the chief of police. All the rest of the policemen would just sort of run from this fellow, because if they didn't, they'd either have to shoot him or get cut themselves.

But Ed Blakeman would always come and talk to him and put him in jail until he sobered up. Then he'd turn him loose. The whole town sympathized with the fellow because he was a veteran in that condition. They realized he wasn't altogether to blame. In fact, he was the finest, most splendid gentleman you ever saw until he would begin to feel bad physically and have those spells because of the war. Then he'd get drunk, and he'd get mean.

One Saturday night he was in a cafe on the east side of the town square, and he was drinking. He pulled his knife on somebody. A policeman was nearby, and he ran out to call Mr. Blakeman. He said, "_____ is on a rampage again. You'd better get down here."

Mr. Blakeman got down there as fast as he could. Meanwhile the owner of the cafe had held the fellow off with a chair and finally pushed him out of the cafe and onto the crowded sidewalk.

It was a Saturday night during the Depression Days, and the sidewalk was very crowded. Immediately, everybody got off the sidewalk because they knew this fellow. They knew he was just liable to cut up anybody he met.

So Mr. Blakeman finally got there, and he met him right on the corner of the square in front of a variety store. He said to him, "Come on, _____, we're going to jail. You're going to sleep this off."

"No," he said, "I'm not going in this time, Ed."

"Yes you are," Mr. Blakeman said.

And this fellow answered, "No, I'm going to cut your throat or you're going to kill me—one of the two." This World War I veteran had just gotten tired of his condition. And in his own mind, I guess he thought, "Well, this is it."

The man attacked Mr. Blakeman, and there wasn't anything he could do but pull his gun. So Mr. Blakeman shot him, and the fellow died as a result.

Everybody felt bad about it in a way. But then again, the whole town almost sighed a sigh of relief. After all, several people had nearly died from being cut up by this fellow.

Yet no one had ever pressed charges against this man because they felt he just wasn't altogether himself. And when he'd go back into the hospital for a while, they'd think he was well enough to get out, and they'd let him out.

When he was killed, everybody talked about it. Some people said, "Well, it's a good riddance. We hated for it to happen that way, but it's just a good riddance."

I remember I went on the job that day, and we were talking about it. And everybody was expressing his opinion about this fellow. But Brother Smith wouldn't say one evil thing about him. I remember hearing him say about the fellow, "Well, one thing about him, he did have pretty eyes."

When Brother Smith said that, I thought, "That fellow did have pretty eyes." So Brother Smith said something good about this man. He wouldn't say anything bad about him. And at 90 years of age, Brother Smith was just as strong as a younger man in every way because he had asked God to help him keep his tongue.

I think some more of us could stand a little of that kind of preaching. *"For he that will love life, and see good days, let him refrain his tongue from evil, and his lips that they speak no guile"* (1 Peter 3:10).

So we can see that the expressions "inward man" and "hidden man of the heart" give us God's definition of the human spirit. And it's with the human spirit or heart of man that man believes. Real faith is of the *heart.*

Two Kinds of Faith

The Bible talks about two kinds of faith—the Thomas-kind of faith or head-faith and the Abraham-kind of faith or heart-faith.

JOHN 20:25–29
25 The other disciples therefore said unto him, We have seen the Lord. But he said unto them, EXCEPT I SHALL SEE in his hands THE PRINT OF THE NAILS, and put my finger into the print of the nails, and THRUST MY HAND INTO HIS SIDE, I WILL NOT BELIEVE.

26 And after eight days again his disciples were within, and Thomas with them: then came Jesus, the doors being shut, and stood in the midst, and said, Peace be unto you.
27 Then saith he to Thomas, Reach hither thy finger, and behold my hands; and reach hither thy hand, and thrust it into my side: and be not faithless, but believing.
28 And Thomas answered and said unto him, My Lord and my God.
29 Jesus saith unto him, Thomas, BECAUSE THOU HAST SEEN ME, THOU HAST BELIEVED: blessed are they that have not seen, and yet have believed.

ROMANS 4:17–21
17 (As it is written, I have made thee a father of many nations,) before him whom he believed, even God, who quickeneth the dead, and calleth those things which be not as though they were.
18 WHO AGAINST HOPE BELIEVED IN HOPE, that he might become the father of many nations, according to that which was spoken, So shall thy seed be.
19 AND BEING NOT WEAK IN FAITH, HE CONSIDERED NOT HIS OWN BODY now dead, when he was about an hundred years old, neither yet the deadness of Sarah's womb:
20 He staggered not at the promise of God through unbelief; but was STRONG IN FAITH, giving glory to God;
21 And being fully persuaded that, what he had promised, he was able also to perform.

The Abraham-kind of faith is the faith that believes in spite of what it sees—in spite of the circumstances. And the Abraham-kind of faith is of the heart. The Thomas-kind of faith believes only what it can see, hear, taste, smell, or touch. The Thomas-kind of faith is head-faith. In other words, it's based on mental reasoning and the senses.

You see, man is a spirit being. He has a soul, and he lives in a body. We contact the physical world with our physical body. We contact the spiritual world with our spirit. And we contact the intellectual world with our soul.

There's only three worlds or realms you live in. Man doesn't contact any other realm except the spiritual, physical, and mental realms, because there's not any more realms than that for him to contact.

But man is actually a spirit being. It helped my faith just to think like that, because faith is of the *heart*, or the spirit, or the inward man. Faith is not of the mind or the body—it's of the heart!

MARK 11:23
23 For verily I say unto you, That whosoever shall say unto this mountain, Be thou removed, and be thou cast into the sea; and shall not doubt IN HIS HEART, but shall believe that those things which he saith shall come to pass; he shall have whatsoever he saith.

Write this down and don't forget it: *Faith will work in your heart with doubt in your head!*

Here's the thing that defeats a lot of Christians. Because they have doubt in their mind, they say, "I'm doubting; I know I am." And, really, whether they mean to or not, they're telling a lie all the time. They just don't know it, because faith will work in your heart with doubt in your head.

Jesus never said a word in the world about not doubting in your head. He said, *"and shall not doubt in his HEART"* (Mark 11:23).

It's heart faith, not head faith, that gets the job done!

Proverbs 3:5 says the same thing.

PROVERBS 3:5
5 Trust in the Lord with all thine HEART; and lean not unto thine own understanding.

Your understanding is your own mental processes—your own human thinking. In other words, you can read that verse like this: "Trust in the Lord with all your heart and lean not to your own mind or human reasoning."

But that's exactly where most Christians miss it. You can give them scriptures, and they will say, "Yes, *but*. . . ." I have people come to me all the time for help, and I have found that the best way in the world to help people is with God's Word.

Put Faith in the Word, Not in Your Feelings

It's not what *we* feel; it's not what *we* think. It's what God's Word says that counts. And our faith should be in what God has said. Our faith shouldn't be in our feelings. We're going to be defeated for certain if our faith is in our feelings.

I remember several years ago I was holding a meeting in Fort Worth, Texas. And at the close of one of the morning services, a woman met me in the aisle and said, "Brother Hagin, I want you to pray for me."

"Well, what for?" I answered.

She said, "Do I have to tell you?"

I said, "Yes, I'm not going to pray unless you do."

"Well," she said, "I'll tell you. I've been saved about seven years now and filled with the Holy Ghost about five years. I've taught Sunday school here in this church for the past five years.

"My husband and I have been married for over twenty years. We weren't Christians when we were married. He never has gotten saved. He always drank a little bit, but he'd just have a drink or two with the fellows. He's never come home drunk. He's a good man and a good husband, and I love him. He's always a good provider, and most of the time, he'll even come to church with me on a Sunday night. But he's never made a move toward God."

She continued: "Before I was saved, I was awfully hot-tempered. But now over a seven-year period, I haven't lost my temper one single time until recently. I've come close a few times. But I've never lost my temper.

"But awhile back, my husband had taken a drink or two, and he came home pretending he was drunk. And I'll just be honest with you, I just got mad. I lost my temper, and I tell you, I turned him every which way but loose. He finally yelled out, 'I'm all right! I'm just putting on—I'm not drunk.'"

And she said, "That made me madder than ever that he played a joke on me and treated me that way. So after I give him another piece of my mind, I went in the bedroom and slammed the door and locked it. And then after two or three hours I cooled off, and I was ashamed of myself. The words I said kept coming back to me. I said a lot of things I shouldn't have said, and I was wrong.

"I got on my knees in the bedroom and just prayed the rest of the night that God would forgive me. I never did open the door and let my husband in. He slept in the other bedroom.

"The next morning at the breakfast table, at first, he didn't say anything to me, and I didn't say anything to him until we sat down to eat. I always prayed over the food, and he'd be very nice about it. He'd always wait for me to pray.

"Finally he said, 'Aren't you going to pray?' I said, 'Before I pray and ask the blessing, I've got to apologize to you. I've prayed and asked God to forgive me, and I want you to forgive me too.'

"'Well,' he answered, 'I don't have anything to forgive you for. I really ought to be asking *you* to forgive *me*. I'm the one who brought it all on. I was the instigator; I'm the one who caused it all. Will you forgive me?'

"I said, 'I'll forgive you, all right. But after all, I'm a Spirit-filled Christian, and I haven't lost my temper in all these seven years. But I lost my temper and said a lot of things I shouldn't have said. I'm wrong, and I want you to forgive me.'

"My husband said, 'All right. I'll forgive you, but I'm to blame for it. You forgive me, too, and go ahead and ask the blessing.' So I stumbled through praying the blessing, and we ate."

I said to her, "Sister, you haven't turned in any prayer request. You've *told* me something."

"Well," she said, "here's what I want you to do. I want you to pray that God would give me some kind of a feeling so I'll know He's forgiven me. I've never felt yet on the inside of me like the Lord's forgiven me."

"Why," I said, "I'm not going to do any such thing. I'm not going to pray one lick about that. You've already got the answer to your problem. The Bible says, *'If we confess our sins, he is faithful and just to forgive us our sins, and to cleanse us from all unrighteousness'"* (1 John 1:9).

"Oh, I know that, Brother Hagin, but . . ."

I said, "Sister, do you know what's wrong with you?"

She said, "No. Do *you?*"

I said, "I certainly do."

She said, "I wished you'd tell me."

I said, "You're not willing to forgive yourself—that's where your trouble is. The Lord forgave you or else He lied about it. And I don't believe He lied. Do you think your husband lied when you asked *him* to forgive you, and he said he would?"

"No," she said, "I don't think he lied."

"Then you have more faith in an unsaved husband than you do in God. God said, 'If we confess our sins, He is faithful and just to forgive us our sins and to cleanse us from all unrighteousness.'"

Then I said, "Do you know what else you're telling me? You're telling me that God may have lied about it, but that your feelings don't lie. Your feelings say God hasn't forgiven you, but God says He has. You can believe your feelings, but you can't believe God."

Scriptural Praying Brings Results

Friends, you can't help people as long as they're taking sides against the Word. You've got to side in with God's Word if you want it to work for you.

A lot of folks don't catch on, but that woman was intelligent enough to get it. And she saw how terrible it was to have more faith in her feelings than in God's Word.

Our faith must not be in our feelings. Our faith must be in what God says.

Sometimes people's prayers are nothing more than lost motion because they are praying unscripturally. If they'd pray and believe God according to the Bible, they could expect an answer every time.

Through the years I've taken a few surveys along this line. And over a period of several years, I'd ask everybody who turned in a prayer request to me personally, "What is your prayer request?" And the majority of the time, they'd say, "Do I have to tell you?" And I'd always say, "Yes. I'm not going to pray unless you do."

You see, it really wouldn't do any good for me to pray if I didn't know what I was praying about. If you want me to pray about something for you, then you're either expecting me to have faith for it, or you're expecting me to agree with you that it'll come to pass.

But how in the world am I going to have faith for something when I don't even know what I'm believing for? I couldn't. And you can't have faith for something when you don't know what you're believing for. You can't agree on something when you don't know what you're agreeing on.

Also, many times people just get in the habit of saying, "Pray for me. Pray for me," and they don't mean a thing in the world by it—it's just words. Those people are just making conversation.

I remember holding a meeting down in east Texas. Several pastors came to one of the day teaching services, and afterwards several of the ministers and I stood around talking. One by one they left, and finally there was just one visiting pastor. He got ready to go, so he shook hands with me, and just before he stepped out the door, he said, "Pray for me."

When he said that, I just held on to his hand and asked, "What for?" When I asked him that, he looked at me sort of startled and batted his eyes like a toad frog in a west Texas hailstorm! He said, "Well, uh, *I don't know.*"

But if you don't know what you're praying for, you won't know whether or not you received it!

If you'll pray scripturally—in line with the Word—you'll get results. And, as I said, faith will work in your heart with doubt in your head.

Some of the greatest things that ever happened to me, happened while I was having trouble with doubts in my head—in my mind. Even in receiving healing for my own body—a body practically totally paralyzed with two serious organic heart troubles and an incurable blood disease—I had a battle with my head the whole time. I began to say, "I believe I receive my healing for my heart." And my head said, "It's not so. It's not so. It's not so. It's not so . . ."

Oh, I had trouble with my head! But faith will work in your heart with doubt in your head. Real Bible-believing faith is of the heart!

We read in John chapter 20 and Romans chapter 4 about the difference between the Thomas-kind of faith and the Abraham-kind of faith. In these two portions of scripture we have a contrast between two kinds of faith—between head faith and heart faith.

Thomas' faith was a head faith, not a heart faith.

You see, after Jesus' resurrection, He appeared to the disciples, and Thomas wasn't with them. And the disciples said to Thomas: "We have seen the Lord" (John 20:25).

Thomas said, "I'll not believe unless I can see the print or the wound of the nail in his hands, put my finger in those nail holes, and see the wound in his side where that soldier took that Roman spear and thrust it under his rib cage in his left side." That Roman spear was said to have been about five inches wide at the base, so there would have been plenty of room for Thomas to put his hand.

The disciples were gathered together in a room when Thomas said this. The door was shut, but suddenly Jesus appeared in their midst and said, "Peace be unto you." And He said to Thomas, *"Reach hither thy finger, and behold my hands; and reach hither thy hand, and thrust it into my side: and be not faithless, but believing"* (John 20:27).

You see, Jesus knew what Thomas had said even though He wasn't physically present that day when Thomas said it.

And Thomas said, "My Lord, and my God" (John 20:28). You see, when Jesus appeared, Thomas believed.

And Jesus said, *"Thomas, because thou hast seen me, thou hast believed"* (John 20:29).

Jesus didn't commend Thomas' kind of faith. He didn't recommend Thomas' kind of faith. In effect, Jesus said, "You only believe because you've seen."

But *anybody* could have that kind of faith—sinner or saint! That's a head faith. That's believing what your physical senses tell your mind.

But Jesus said, *"blessed are they that have not seen, and yet have believed"* (John 20:29).

Calling Those Things That Be Not as Though They Were

Let's look again in Romans at God's own account of Abraham and his faith.

ROMANS 4:18–21

18 Who against hope believed in hope, that he might become the father of many nations, according to that which was spoken, So shall thy seed be.

19 And being not weak in faith, he considered not his own body now dead, when he was about an hundred years old, neither yet the deadness of Sarah's womb:

20 He staggered not at the promise of God through unbelief; but was strong in faith, giving glory to God;

21 And being fully persuaded that, what he had promised, he was able also to perform.

Paul, inspired by the Spirit of God, wrote these words. You can read an account of this back in Genesis 17. When Abram was ninety-nine years old, the Lord God appeared to Abram and said, *"Neither shall thy name any more be called Abram, but thy name shall be Abraham; for a father of many nations HAVE I MADE THEE"* (Gen. 17:5).

Now get this, because God said, "The father of many nations *have I made* thee."

Think on that a little bit. I know it's different than human reasoning and human thinking. You'll have to meditate on it a little bit for it to dawn on you.

Look at Romans 4:17 again. It says, *"before him whom he believed, even God, who quickeneth the dead, AND CALLETH THOSE THINGS WHICH BE NOT AS THOUGH THEY WERE."*

Notice, God didn't say, "I am *going* to make you the father of many nations." He said, "I *have made* you the father of many nations."

Faith Is *Now*

Faith is always present tense. These people who are always *going* to get something, never get it. They say, "I'm *going* to get the baptism of the Holy Ghost *sometime*."

I know people who have been "*going* to get" something from God for years, and they've never gotten it yet. They've said, "I believe I'm *going* to get my healing sometime." I know people like that who are still sick and some who have died.

A man once told me, "I believe I'll get saved sometime." Bless his darling heart, I tried to get him to accept his salvation *now*. The Bible says, *"NOW is the accepted time; behold, now is the day of salvation"* (2 Cor. 6:2). But this man eventually died and went to hell. And right now while you're reading this book, he's in hell "lifting up his eyes in torment" (Luke 16:23).

Yet this man said to me, "I'm not planning on going to hell. I'm going to get saved *sometime.*" But he didn't. He's in hell today.

That's not faith. You may call it "believing," but it isn't even believing. It is really just hope.

HEBREWS 11:1
1 NOW faith is the substance of things hoped for, the evidence of things not seen.

This verse says, *"Now* faith *is."* If it's not now, it's not faith. Faith is *now*—it's present tense.

Now notice in Romans 4:17 that Abraham believed God. It says, *"before him whom he* [Abraham] *believed, even God, who quickeneth the dead, and calleth those things which be not as though they were."*

What did Abraham believe?

ROMANS 4:18
18 Who against hope believed in hope, that he might become the father of many nations, ACCORDING TO THAT WHICH WAS SPOKEN, So shall thy seed be.

Abraham believed according to that which was spoken. He didn't believe according to what he could *see*. He didn't believe according to what he could *feel*. He didn't believe according to what his physical senses told him. He didn't believe according to what his mind told him. Abraham believed according to what God said.

Well, if Abraham believed according to what was spoken, what exactly did he believe then? He didn't believe he was *going* to be a father, because God didn't say He was *going* to make Abraham the father of many nations.

No, Abraham believed that God had already done it—that God *had already made* him the father of many nations because that's what God had said. If Abraham believed according to that which was spoken, then he believed that he *had been made* the father of many nations.

You see, faith calls those things which be not as though they were. That's what causes them to come into being!

I've had people tell me, "Yes, Brother Hagin, but common sense will tell you such and such." I said, "I know it, but where did you ever read in the Bible where it said, 'We walk by common sense'?

"You never read that anywhere. The Bible said, 'We walk by faith and not by sight'" (2 Cor. 5:7). You see, common sense is based on sight—on what your physical senses tell you.

For instance, common sense will tell you that a man a hundred years old and a woman ninety years old are not going to become a mamma and papa. But Abraham didn't walk by common sense. He trusted the Lord with all his heart and leaned *not* to his own understanding (Prov. 3:5).

He believed according to that which was spoken. I don't know about you, but that has brought me through many a hard place. I just stood my ground and looked at the opposition—at all the circumstances that contradicted what I was believing for and told me I didn't have my answer. And I said from my heart, "I believe according to that which was spoken."

My feelings said, "You don't have the answer." My sight said, "No, you don't have it." But I said from my heart, "I believe according to that which was spoken in God's Word. It is written, and that's what I believe."

I'm not moved by what I see; I'm not moved by what I feel. I'm moved *only* by what I believe. And what a difference that makes.

When I can get folks to act on God's Word, it's the simplest thing in the world to get people healed.

Yes, I believe in gifts of the Spirit. I believe in praying with an anointing of the Spirit. There are various ways of ministering healing by the Spirit, and those ways will work for some people some of the time because the gifts of the Spirit are manifested as the Holy Spirit wills (1 Cor. 12:11). But God's Word will *always* work for anyone who dares to believe and act on it.

I remember I was ministering in the state of Oklahoma several years ago (we lived in Texas at the time). I met some preachers I'd known in Texas who had moved to Oklahoma. They were pastors now.

One of the pastors told me: "Brother Hagin, we're going to bring a lady from our church who's crippled and can't walk a step. She's

72 years old and she hasn't walked a step in the last four years. The doctor has said she'll never walk again."

They brought her to the meeting, and I was ministering each night with an anointing of healing power. But we had a lot of people to pray for, and when you're praying for a lot of folks, after a while the anointing will sort of lift from you.

So by the time I got to this woman, the anointing was gone. Well, I knew then that I couldn't minister to her with the healing anointing. The people who brought her to the meeting came from a distance and they couldn't bring her back, so this was the only time I could minister to her.

So I said, "Just sit her down here, and I'll minister to her." As I began ministering to her, among other things, I said to her, "Sister, did you know that you *are* healed?"

I remember she looked at me, and her eyes got big, because here she was sitting there crippled and hadn't walked a step in four years. Her doctor was a specialist, and he had said, "She'll never walk another step the longest day she lives."

When I said, "Sister, did you know you are healed?" she said, "Oh, am I?"

I said, "You sure are. You *are* healed. You're not *going* to be healed—you are! And I'll prove that to you by the Bible."

I opened my Bible to First Peter 2:24 and laid it on her lap. I said to her, "Would you mind reading verse 24 out loud?" And she read aloud, *"Who his own self bare our sins in his own body on the tree, that we, being dead to sins, should live unto righteousness: by whose stripes ye WERE healed"* (1 Peter 2:24).

Then I said, "May I ask you a question?"

She said, "You may."

I said, "Notice, that last clause said, *"by whose stripes ye WERE healed.* Is 'were' past tense, future tense, or present tense?"

"Why," she said, "it's past tense." Then she said, "If we *were* healed, then I *was* healed!"

You see, if you're going to believe what God said about healing, this is what you're going to believe: You've got to believe that we *were* healed and that you *were* healed.

"Yeah," someone said, "but I'm still sick."

Well, you're not believing it then. You've gone back to believing what your head tells you. You see, a minute before, you said from your heart, "I believe God's Word." But then you slipped right back over to what your head told you, and you said, "No, I don't have it." You turned right back around and started walking by *sight* instead of by *faith*!

When this elderly woman said, "If we *were* healed, then I *was* healed," I said, "That's right! That's right!"

Then before her mind could take over, I said to her real quickly, "Will you do what I tell you?" I knew Satan would try to put a doubt in her mind and try to take over and dominate her through her mind. Then she would say, "Well, if I was healed, then how come I can't walk? How come I'm still crippled? How come my healing isn't here?"

So I said, "Will you do what I tell you?"

She said, "I will if it's easy."

(Everybody's always looking for something easy!) I said to her, "It's the easiest thing you ever did in your life."

I said, "Just lift both of your hands and begin to praise God because you *are* healed. You're not *going* to be—you *are*!"

I wish you could have seen that dear woman. As simply as a little child, she lifted her hands, and her face lit up like a neon sign in the dark. She shut her eyes and turned her head upward to Heaven and said, "Oh, dear Lord, ohhh! I'm so glad I'm healed! Oh! I'm so glad I can walk again."

She hadn't walked a step yet. But, you see, she was talking out of her heart. She believed what the Word says. She believed according to that which is written—that which is spoken—that by Jesus' stripes she *was* healed!

This dear woman continued: "Lord, You know how tired I got sitting around those four years, helpless. I'm so glad I'm healed and can walk again." You see, she'd gotten it in the right tense now. God's Word works for you when you get it in the right tense.

I turned to the congregation and said, "Let's all lift our hands and praise God with her because she *is* healed." And we all lifted our hands.

The woman continued to say, "Thank You, Lord. I'm so glad I'm no longer helpless. I'm so glad I don't have to be waited on anymore. I'm so glad I can wait on myself. I'm so glad my knees are well. I'm so glad my limbs are well. I'm so glad I'm no longer crippled."

We all praised God with her a few moments, and then I turned to her and said, "Now my Sister, arise and walk!" and I just held my hand out to her.

Instantly, God and about 500 people as my witness, she leapt to her feet! She leapt to her feet, and she sat back down real quickly, and then she jumped up again. She'd sit down, and she'd jump up. She was completely healed!

I'll tell you, most 72-year-old folks couldn't have done that if they *hadn't* been crippled. But this woman was jumping up and down.

Then she ran over a few steps and stood there and danced a little jig for joy. For about 10 minutes she'd run, dance for joy, and come back and sit down in the same place. Then she'd jump up again. We all just shouted and laughed and cried with her.

This dear woman had been sitting around four years and hadn't walked a step. She was helpless, and the doctor said she'd never walk again. But here she was walking and jumping and leaping like the healed man who went into the temple walking and leaping and praising God (Acts 3:8).

And then somebody went off and lied on me, saying, "You know, that fellow Hagin healed a crippled woman over there at the church last night."

I never had a thing in the world to do with that woman's healing! I never had anymore to do with it than you could have had to do with it. All I did was just bring her the Word, and the Word did it!

That elderly woman just found out what belonged to her—what had been hers all the time. Really, in the mind of God, she was healed all those four years she had been sitting around crippled. But she never believed it before. She didn't get her believing in the right tense. All that time she had been *seeking* healing.

Afterward, another dear woman in the same church came to me afterward and said, "Brother Hagin, that crippled woman got healed. Why won't God heal me?"

Bless her heart. I feel so sorry for folks like that because I see they've never caught on to what's going on. I feel so sorry I could cry. Very often I get in my car and drive away from a service weeping because folks have never caught on to what you're talking about.

So many of them close their minds and don't continue to meditate on God's Word, and God's Word can't go down on the inside of them because they won't let it.

This woman had been prayed for several times. I had prayed for her and laid hands on her more than once myself. And she asked, "Why won't God heal me?"

I said, "Now Sister, God's done all He's ever going to do about healing you."

"Oh, you mean God's not going to heal me?"

I said, "I didn't say that." I said, "He's done all He's ever going to do about healing you."

"You mean He's not going to heal me?"

I said, "I didn't say that." I said, "He's already done something about your healing. He's already purchased your healing for you. That scripture—the same verse I gave to that crippled woman—said, *'by whose stripes ye WERE healed'*" (1 Peter 2:24).

"Well, I'll tell you what *I* think about it," she said.

I said, "I know you will. And that's what's got you in the mess you're in. You're going by what *you* think about it instead of what *God* said about it."

"Well," she said, "I'm going to keep on praying. I believe that sometime, somewhere, some way, God's going to heal me."

I said, "No, He isn't! I know He isn't because He *already has*! Certainly, I know the manifestation will come sometime if you'll believe it. But you've got to believe in the right tense because God already *has* healed you!"

God's Word *is*! Faith *is*! Faith is present tense: *Now* faith *is* (Heb. 11:1)!

And faith is of the heart, not the head. Remember Jesus said, *"and shall not doubt in his HEART, but shall believe that those things which he saith shall come to pass; he shall have whatsoever he saith"* (Mark 11:23).

I'll say it again because it bears repeating: *Faith will work in your heart with doubt in your head.* And I want to reemphasize that that's what defeats so many Christians. In other words, because there's a doubt in their mind, they say, "Oh, I'm doubting, and I know I am. If I said I wasn't doubting, I'd be lying about it. And I'm not a liar." Yet they're lying about it all the time and don't even know it because faith will work in your heart with doubt in your head!

Follow Abraham's Example of Faith

One preacher said to me, "Yes, Brother Hagin, but I'm not going to believe I've got something my physical senses don't tell me I have. I'm not going to believe I've got something I can't see."

I said, "Do you believe you've got any brains?"

"Why, certainly," he said.

I said, "Did you ever see them?"

"Oh," he said. "That's *different.*"

"How come that's different? I thought you weren't going to believe you had anything you couldn't see?"

Abraham believed he had something he couldn't see. Thomas wouldn't do it. Abraham believed "according to that which was spoken" (Rom. 4:18). He didn't believe according to what he could see like Thomas did (John 20:25). Abraham's faith was a heart-faith, not a head-faith.

ROMANS 4:17

17 (As it is written, I have made thee a father of many nations,) before him whom he believed, even God, who quickeneth the dead, and calleth those things which be not as though they were.

God is a faith God, and we're faith children of a faith God!

One person said to me: "Well, it would be all right for God to call those things which be not as though they were because He's *God*. But it would be wrong for me to do it."

I said, "If it's wrong for you to do it, it's wrong for God to do it. I mean, children of the devil act like the devil. Shouldn't children of God act like *God*?"

Sure they should! God's a faith God. And we're faith children of a faith God. And because we're faith children of a faith God, we're to act in faith. And faith calls those things which be not as though they were!

One woman said, "Yes, Brother Hagin. I know that's true, all right. But now, I'll tell you what my trouble is. . ."

(You know, one trouble with some folks is they diagnose their own case instead of letting the Bible diagnose it. They think they know exactly where the trouble is.)

"What is your trouble?" I asked the woman.

She answered, "I just don't have any faith."

I said, "Then why don't you get saved?"

"Oh, I am saved!"

"Then if you're saved," I said, "you've got faith."

"But I know I don't."

I said, "You or God is lying about it then, because God plainly said in Ephesians 2:8: *'For by grace are ye saved through faith; and that not of yourselves: it is the gift of God.'*

"So if you're saved and don't have faith, then God told a lie on you. He says you have faith, and you say you don't."

"Well," this woman said, "I guess I have faith, all right. But my trouble is, I'm so *weak* in faith. I just wish you'd pray for me that I'd grow stronger in faith."

"No," I said, "I'm not going to do that. In fact, to tell you the real truth about it, Sister, you are strong in faith. You just don't know it."

"Well, I know I'm not. I tell you, I'm just about the weakest one of the bunch."

I said, "May I ask you a question? Now I'm not trying to be a smart aleck. I just want to ask you a simple question."

"Why, sure," she said.

I said, "All right. Are you fully persuaded that whatever God's promised you, He's able to perform?"

"Why, certainly," she said. "I know God can do anything. And anything He said He'd do, He can do it, and He will do it! I *know* that."

I said, "I want to ask you another question. Can you say, 'Glory to God' or 'Praise God' and praise God's Word for it?"

"Why, certainly. I do that every day."

"Well," I said, "you're strong in faith then."

"No, I'm not."

I said, "Well, wait a minute, Sister. Can you read?"

"Yes, I can read."

I said, "Look here at Romans 4:20 and 21. It tells you what strong faith is.

"It said, *'He* [Abraham] *staggered not at the promise of God through unbelief; but was STRONG IN FAITH, GIVING GLORY TO GOD; And being FULLY PERSUADED that, what he had promised, he was able also to perform.'"

This woman had faith all along but she wasn't enjoying the benefits of her faith. She was walking by her senses—by her feelings—instead of by what the Bible said.

Our faith should not be in our feelings. What we feel or think about a situation is not what's important. What's important is what God's Word says about it. That's why we should meditate and feed our spirit man on God's Word. The real faith that comes by hearing God's Word will produce results for us. And real Bible faith is of the heart.

Chapter Four

Forgive and Keep a Good Report

I'm teaching on the seven most important things about faith. First, we learned that every believer has a measure of the God-kind of faith—the kind of faith that created the worlds in the beginning—the mountain-moving faith!

Second, we learned that your faith can grow and develop. But it's your responsibility, not God's, to see to it that your faith grows.

Third, we saw that real Bible faith is of the heart, not the head or the mind. It's with the *heart* that man believes.

I also said that Mark 11:23 and 24 contain some of the most astounding things Jesus ever said about faith. Yet we can't study this all-important subject of faith without studying the entire context of Mark 11:23 and 24.

MARK 11:22–26
22 And Jesus answering saith unto them, Have faith in God.
23 For verily I say unto you, That whosoever shall say unto this mountain, Be thou removed, and be thou cast into the sea; and shall not doubt in his heart, but shall believe that those things which he saith shall come to pass; he shall have whatsoever he saith.
24 Therefore I say unto you, What things soever ye desire, when ye pray, believe that ye receive them, and ye shall have them.
25 And when ye stand praying, forgive, if ye have ought against any: that your Father also which is in heaven may forgive you your trespasses.
26 But if ye do not forgive, neither will your Father which is in heaven forgive your trespasses.

The fourth most important thing about faith is, *faith will not work when there is an air of unforgiveness about you.* Jesus said in Mark 11:25, *"And when ye stand praying, FORGIVE."*

As I said, in Mark 11:23 and 24 Jesus made these marvelous statements on the subject of faith that are very thrilling, amazing, and astounding. Those are marvelous statements, and no one's ever plumbed the depths of those statements yet. But at the same time—at the same scene and with the same breath—Jesus also said, "And when you stand praying, *forgive.*"

Faith Can Be Hindered

If there's a spirit of unforgiveness about you or an air of unforgiveness about you, your faith won't work. Your prayers won't work. Of all the statements Jesus made about faith (and you can read them in the four Gospels), unforgiveness is the only hindrance Jesus ever mentioned. Therefore, it must be of primary importance.

I tell people all the time, "If my prayers and my faith didn't work, *this would be the first place I'd look!"* In other words, I just never will permit anything in my mind at all that's against somebody else. I refuse to think anything bad about anyone. I don't care what they do to me or what they say about me, I never permit it to affect me because if I do, it'll affect my faith.

I remember years ago as a Baptist boy preacher, I was the pastor of a community church. We made it a community church because it was a country church, the only one in the community, and everybody came to that church. About 85 percent of us were Southern Baptists, and about 15 percent were from other denominations. Some of the finest men in the community were in our church.

Then I received the baptism of the Holy Ghost, and we all went Pentecostal. About 93 percent of the folks followed me in. And then sometime later I changed over and accepted the pastorate of a Full-Gospel church, because way back in 1937, if you got to talking in tongues, you were "out." So after pastoring this community church for about three years, I accepted the pastorate of the Full Gospel church.

A woman in this Full Gospel congregation came to the parsonage one day after I'd been pastoring there three or four months. She and my wife and I talked for a while, and she said, "Brother Hagin, I have a question I want to ask you."

Well, you know, most folks are full of questions, so I said, "You can ask it, but I don't know whether I can answer it or not. If I can answer it, I will. If I can't, I'll tell you I can't."

She said, "I know you've only been here about three or four months as pastor, but you've been here long enough to find out some things. I've only been a Christian about eight or nine months, so I'm just a baby Christian. But my mother, one of my sisters, and some of the rest of the family have been in this church for 23 years.

"You know since you've been here that there's not anybody any more faithful a Christian than Mamma and some of our family. They never miss a service."

I said, "Yes," and she said, "Well, they've been just that consistent over a 23-year period. They've always put in their tithes and have helped support the church."

This woman's mother *was* a very spiritual woman. She had various gifts of the Spirit in manifestation in her life at times. And I'll be perfectly honest with you—in all the 12 years I pastored, I considered her to be one of the most spiritual and gifted persons I ever pastored. I saw more manifestations of the Spirit in her life than any other person I'd ever met, including about eight out of ten preachers I know. She was a very dedicated and consecrated woman of God.

I said to this woman, "I agree with you that your mother and your sister, too, as far as I'm concerned, are very faithful. There's not anybody who's any more consecrated and dedicated to the work of God than your family."

Then I said to her, "But you haven't asked me any question; you've just *told* me something, and I agree with you."

She continued: "You didn't know my husband's family, but his family have also been in this church over a 23-year period. His mother lived her time out and went home to be with Jesus as an elderly woman. And some of the rest of the family have moved away, so you only know my husband."

She said, "My husband's family and my family have been in this church over a period of 23 years. My family is the most faithful and dedicated and consecrated and separated. My husband's family was saved and filled with the Holy Spirit, all right, and they were good people. For example, they wouldn't tell a lie for anything in the world.

"But they were just about the most unfaithful people you've ever seen in your life. You couldn't depend on them for a thing in the world when it came to church work. They wouldn't even come to the services. Then one of them might show up for three or four weeks. Then they'd stop coming again for a while. They never did put a dime in to support the church when they did come back" (her husband, however, was very faithful about paying his tithes).

She continued: "Just about the time you thought my husband's family were going to stay in church and go all out for the Lord, they'd get out of church and wouldn't come for a while. Then about the time you thought they were out of church for good, they'd started coming again."

I said, "You still haven't asked me anything. You've *told* me something."

"Here's my question," she said. "Over this 23-year period, if anybody in my family ever got healed, I don't know it. We were the ones who always ended up having to go to the hospital and being operated on or dying early." Two of her family members had died prematurely.

"But in my husband's family," she continued, "if any one of them ever *failed* to get healed, I don't know it.

"Brother Hagin, can you explain that to me?"

That was a pretty big question! I said to her, "Sister, I don't know why one person gets healed and another one doesn't. And no one else would know for sure specifically unless God revealed it to him. So I wouldn't really know unless God revealed it to me, and He hasn't."

Let me give you a little side thought here about this. One time when the Lord appeared to me in a vision, I asked Him about one of my loved ones who failed to receive healing and had to have a very serious operation. In the vision, Jesus was talking to me about something else, and then I asked Him about my loved one.

I had prayed so earnestly and used all the faith I had for this family member. I asked Jesus, "Why did she not receive healing and have to have this operation?" She was a born again, Spirit-filled, very consecrated, dedicated Christian.

The Lord Jesus said to me: "That's between Me and her. It isn't any of your business." I mean, He was just as plain as could be about it. He said, "It isn't any of your business."

You see, we're always going around trying to tend to somebody else's business. But the Lord said, "It is My business and her business, not yours."

Then Jesus said to me: "Did you ever read in My Word where it said, *'The secret things belong unto the Lord our God: but those things which are revealed belong unto us and to our children for ever'?"*

I said, "Yes, that's Deuteronomy 29:29."

"Well," He said, "why your family member didn't get healed is a secret between Me and her. If I'd wanted you to know, I would have told you. And if I don't tell you, just don't even think about it. Don't even touch it in your thought life.

"But what's revealed to you, you preach. Go ahead and preach healing just like you're preaching it because it's right. But if people don't get healed, don't even think about it. Don't even touch it in thought life. It isn't any of your business. You're not healing them anyway; you're just preaching it."

Since then, I don't even think about it when folks don't get healed. That's what the Lord told me to do, so that's what I do.

I said to the woman who asked me why her family never got healed, "I don't know why some folks get healed and others don't unless the Lord shows me. But I do know some general rules that are laid down in God's Word. So without knowing your husband's family, I would say that they had two outstanding characteristics. I would say that they were quick *to repent and to forgive* and that they were quick *to believe*."

I didn't have any specific revelation on it, but I do know the Bible. And about nine times out of ten, you'll always get your answer in the Word, not through some special prophesy or Word from the Lord.

When I said that, I remember her eyes got almost as big as saucers! She said, "Brother Hagin, you've hit the nail right on the head!"

"No" I said. "I didn't hit the nail on the head—the Word did. I got that out of the Word."

She said, "I believe my husband's family were the quickest people I've ever seen in my life to forgive. If they thought they had hurt or offended you in any way, they would repent and ask you to forgive them. And they thoroughly meant it.

"Also, they could be out of church the longest, and then come to church, go to the altar, repent the fastest, believe God the quickest, and get blessed more than anybody I've ever seen in my lifetime.

"But now," she said, "you take Mamma and the rest of us, and I'll tell you, we would hardly forgive anybody. It's a characteristic with the whole family. Oh, we would eventually forgive because we knew we had to because the Bible says so. But we'd hold out as long as we could.

"And when it comes to believing, it's the hardest thing in the world for us to believe anything."

That would be funny if it wasn't so pathetic. I said, "You've answered your own question." She said, "I guess I have."

Our text said, *"When you stand praying, FORGIVE"* (Mark 11:25). If you want your faith to work, you'll forgive.

You *Can* Forgive

"Yes," someone said, "I believe that, all right, but I just can't do it."

One lady said to me, "Brother Hagin, I just wish you'd cast this old unforgiving spirit out of me. I've got something against a lady here in the church, and I've tried and tried, but I can't forgive her. I just don't seem to have the ability to forgive."

"Well" I said, "I'm going to ask you a question, Sister. Have you ever had to forgive your husband for anything?"

"Oh, yes," she said. "I've had to forgive him, and he has had to forgive me too."

I said, "You can forgive your husband? I thought you couldn't forgive."

She laughed and said, "You know, I can, can't I!"

I said, "Sure. If you can forgive one person, you can forgive another one."

Friends, it's that simple. Many times we complicate matters needlessly. For example, notice what Jesus said: *"When you stand praying, forgive"* (Mark 11:25).

That means you can forgive. Jesus didn't tell you to do something you couldn't do. If He told you to do something you couldn't do, He'd be unjust. But He's not unjust.

You see, a lot of times people just don't want to go to the trouble to do something. They want somebody else to do it for them when, really, it's their responsibility.

Once after a meeting I was holding, a minister's wife said to me, "Brother Hagin, hearing you preach and teach, you've gotten me confused."

"No, Sister," I said. "I haven't gotten you confused. You were confused when I came here; the light of God's Word just showed it up."

You know, you can take a flashlight and go down in a basement or up in the attic where you store things. There could be dust and dirt everywhere, but you wouldn't say, "My! Look what that flashlight's done"! No, that dust was there all the time—the flashlight didn't put the dust there. The flashlight just showed it up.

This minister's wife said, "I'm in an awful shape."

"Why?" I asked.

"Because I can't forgive my mother-in-law, I just hate her. I *hate* my mother-in-law."

I said, "You can't forgive her?"

"No," she said. "I can't."

She continued: "Brother Hagin, you used that scripture that says, *'Whosoever HATETH HIS BROTHER is a murderer: and ye know that no murderer hath eternal life abiding in him'* (1 John 3:15). Then after you said, 'hateth his brother,' you said, 'That means *mother-in-law* too.'

"Now I don't even know whether I'm saved or not because I hate my mother-in-law."

I just let her keep talking and getting a little deeper in trouble before I got her out.

I said, "According to the scripture, if you hate your mother-in-law, you're not saved. It's just that plain and simple."

"Oh, my," she said. "I don't know what in the world I'm going to do, because I've just got an unforgiving spirit about me. I just can't forgive her, and I hate her. I'm in an awful shape."

Well, I could understand why some things were the way they were, because I'd met the family. This woman's husband was an only boy. He had two or three sisters, and his daddy died when he was a little boy, about five or six years old.

This mother and these sisters had raised this boy. And then because he was the only boy, as he grew up into manhood, all these women would boss him. But when he got married, his wife wanted to have some say in his life too. So there was a conflict.

So now that this man was married, his wife wanted to tell him what to do, but his mother was still wanting to tell him what to do. So he's between a rock and a hard place, so to speak. I could understand how the situation could be so difficult.

But I also knew that from her heart, this woman didn't hate her mother-in-law. She was saved and filled with the Holy Spirit. She was just letting the devil dominate her through her mind and flesh.

The Love of God Is Shed Abroad in Our Heart

This woman had begun to doubt whether she ever had anything from God or not. I said to her, "Sister, look me right in the eye and say out loud, 'I hate my mother-in-law,' and then check up on the inside of you, in your spirit. The Bible says the love of God has been shed abroad in our hearts, not our heads (Rom. 5:5). When you say, 'I hate my mother-in-law,' tell me what's going on inside of you."

So she looked me right in the face and said, "I hate my mother-in-law."

I asked, "What happened on the inside?"

She said, "There's something scratching me down there."

I said, "Yes, I know. You see, there's something on the inside of you that's trying to get your attention, because the love of God within you wants to dominate you. But you're letting your head dominate you. That's where the problem is—it's in your head—in your mind."

She said, "I believe you're right."

I said, "Sure I am. It's the Bible. From your heart, you love everybody, don't you?"

"Yes," she said, "I believe I do."

"But," I said, "in your mind, you've let all of these things that have happened affect you. Now you've got to let your heart dominate you, not your head."

A few nights later this minister's wife invited Oretha and me to her house for refreshments after the evening service. She had also invited her husband's mother and sisters and their families. Previously, this minister's wife wouldn't have anything to do with them because she resented them.

–100–

We went to her house after the service and had a splendid time. I remember she whispered to my wife and me, "You know, I don't hate my in-laws; I love them. You were exactly right—the love of God was in my heart all the time. I was just letting my head dominate me because of things that happened in the past."

The mother-in-law was saved and filled with the Spirit, too, but she was letting the natural dominate her too. Sometimes if a mother just has one boy, she thinks there's no girl in all the world who's good enough for her boy. And she doesn't mind expressing herself sometimes, which doesn't help a lot!

This minister's wife said to me, "You know, I found out that my husband's family are lovely people. I was all wrong, and you were right. The confusion was all in my head, and it was there before you ever got here. But God's Word got me all straightened out."

Mountain-Moving Faith Works by Love

Now I'm going to share with you a secret that will help you that will illustrate that your faith will work for you when you forgive and keep a good report.

This minister's wife and her husband had three children. They had one child of their own—their oldest child—and they had adopted two more through the years. The youngest child they'd adopted was a little girl. When they took her as a baby, the doctor said, "We've examined her, and as far as we can ascertain, she's in perfect health."

And for the first two and a half years, there wasn't a thing wrong with the child. She seemed to be a perfect child physically. But then at about two and a half years old, she began to have some kind of spells. Her parents took her to the doctor, and they finally went to the leading specialist in their region, and he said, "Her seizures are epileptic. Your daughter has epilepsy."

After running a brain-wave test on the child, the doctor said, "I'm a specialist in this area of medicine, and in the United States I'm considered to be one of the leading experts concerning this disease. I don't do anything else except treat epilepsy and other related diseases. And in all my years of practicing medicine, this is the worst case of epilepsy I've ever seen."

The parents had the child on medication. She would still have spells, but they wouldn't be as bad because she was constantly on medication. And so, of course, this minister's wife wanted her child to be healed. The child had been prayed for, and not because the mother was told to do so, but because of the mother's own faith, she seemed to be led to take the child off her medication. And the child was doing fine.

The child went for days with no symptoms whatsoever. But then one day, the mother called us and said, "Brother Hagin, would you and Oretha come pray for my daughter. She's having a spell."

Before the little girl would go into this main epileptic seizure, there would be a little preliminary attack, and that's what she was having. So we went to their house.

On the way over there, the Lord spoke to me and said, "Don't pray at all for the child. Tell her mother that in the Old Testament I said to Israel, 'You keep My statutes and My commandments, and I'll take sickness away from the midst of thee and the number of your days you'll fulfill'" (Exod. 23:25–26). (The Lord said that to the Israelites more than once.)

The Lord continued: "You tell her that under the New Covenant, the New Testament only has one commandment. I said, '*A new commandment I give unto you, That ye love one another; as I have loved you, that ye also love one another*'" (John 13:34).

"Oh," somebody said, "you mean we don't have to keep the Ten Commandments?" Well, the new commandment is love. And if you love me, you don't have to say, "Thou shalt not lie about Brother Hagin." If you love me, you're not going to lie about me. If you love me, you're not going to steal from me.

You see, if you walk in the law of love, you'll never violate any rule that was given to curb sin. You don't have to worry about any other commandments, because if you're walking in love, you'll automatically keep all those commandments. It's just that simple.

Jesus made other reference to the new commandment of love.

JOHN 13:35
35 By this shall all men know that ye are my disciples, if ye have love one to another.

1 JOHN 3:14
14 We know that we have passed from death unto life, because we love the brethren. He that loveth not his brother abideth in death.

On the way over to this woman's house, Jesus said to me through the Holy Spirit: "You tell her that if she keeps My commandment of love under the New Covenant, I'll take sickness away from the midst of her and the number of her days she'll fulfill."

When we arrived at her home, I said that to her. I said, "I'm not going to pray at all. You're walking in love now. You've got all that straightened out between your mother-in-law and your sisters-in-law, and you're walking in love. So I'm not going to pray at all, and the child's not going to have an attack. As long as you walk in love, there'll be no sickness here."

While we were yet talking, the little preliminary attack left the child. We stayed on in that city for three more weeks of meetings, and she never had any more symptoms or any kind of attack.

Before when the child would have these attacks, it seemed as if she was almost like a retarded child. She never was that way until she started having these attacks. But during the attacks, her coordination wasn't right and her eyes looked dull.

But five years later when the child was eight or nine years old, we were visiting their home again, and we saw this girl. She had the highest IQ of anybody in her class. She was making straight A's on everything. Her eyes looked bright, and she was lively and full of life.

We asked the mother, "Did she ever have another attack?" She said, "No, to this day, she's never had another one. Only one time did she begin to have that preliminary attack, but I just said, 'Oh, no, devil, you can't put that on my child. I'm walking in love, and I've got God's Word for it. So long as I keep His commandment of love, He'll take sickness away from the midst of us and the number of our days we'll fulfill.' When I said that, the attack stopped in an instant, just like you snapped your finger."

Praise God, that girl is grown and married now with a family of her own.

If you're not walking in love and forgiving others as the Word commands, it would do you well to get rid of unforgiveness and to walk in love. Faith works by love (Gal. 5:6), and love never fails. When you forgive and keep a good report, your faith will produce results and move mountains for you.

Chapter Five

Faith Must Be Released

The 'Saying' Part of Faith

For verily I say unto you, That whosoever shall say unto this mountain, Be thou removed, and be thou cast into the sea; and shall not doubt in his heart, but shall believe that those things which he saith shall come to pass; he shall have whatsoever he saith.

—Mark 11:23

Notice, Jesus concluded Mark 11:23 by saying, *"he shall have whatsoever he SAITH."* The fifth most important thing you should know about faith is that *faith must be released in word through your mouth.*

I remember many years ago I was holding a revival meeting in a little town in Texas. It was my custom in those days during all of my meetings to have two fast-days a week. I would always fast on Tuesdays and Thursdays.

Incidentally, concerning fasting, somebody asked me: "Brother Hagin, do you fast much? What is the longest you've ever fasted?" I said, "I've never fasted more than three days at a time in my life. You see, you need to have some purpose in your fast, and I always got my answer within three days."

But those Tuesdays and Thursdays I set aside during my meetings were just days I spent, not to get any specific answer, but just to wait on God. For instance, if I ate an evening meal, I fasted for the next twenty-four hours. I did drink water, but I ate no food.

And I got further with God and made more spiritual progress fasting two days a week than any other way in all of my life. And then, finally, the Lord spoke to me to stop doing that because holding meetings with two services a day and fasting two days make you tired after a while!

The Lord spoke to me and said, "I'm more pleased with your living a fasted life than I am with your having set days to fast."

I said, "Lord, what do You mean, 'living a *fasted life*'?"

"Well," He said, "fasting's not going to change Me, because I'll be the same when you *start* fasting, *while* your fasting, and when you *get through* fasting. I won't change. Your fasting won't change Me.

"*But*," He said, "fasting *will* help you keep the flesh under. You can keep your flesh under all the time and not eat all you want."

So for years during most of my meetings, I would just eat one meal a day in the middle of the day and then occasionally maybe a little something light after church.

Back when I would fast on Tuesdays and Thursdays during my meetings, I spent one of those days in the church building for nearly the entire day, reading the Bible, walking around the altar and up and down the aisles of the sanctuary praying and waiting on God, or meditating on His Word.

And I would frequently read the whole Book of Mark. It didn't take long—there's only sixteen chapters. So I would read the whole Book of the Gospel according to St. Mark.

I don't know why, but Mark's always been my favorite Gospel. I guess the reason is that Mark chapter 11 brought me off the bed of sickness as a Baptist boy with two serious organic heart troubles, a body practically totally paralyzed, and an incurable blood disease.

So I was reading the Book of Mark, kneeling at the altar. And I'd read through to chapter 16. And I read there at the end where Jesus said, *"And these signs shall follow them that believe; In my name shall they cast out devils; they shall speak with new tongues; They shall take up serpents; and if they drink any deadly thing, it shall not hurt them; they shall lay hands on the sick, and they shall recover"* (Mark 16:17–18).

I stopped reading and got off my knees and sat down on the floor in front of the altar bench. I was meditating on what Jesus said: *"These signs shall follow them that believe."* That's what I was thinking about. I wasn't thinking about Mark 11—that was the furthest thing from my mind.

As I was sitting there meditating, finally, I just laid down on the floor and continued to meditate on Mark chapter 16. In the Old Testament the Scripture says, *"Be still, and know that I am God"* (Ps. 46:10).

Well, I just got to the place where my mind got quiet, and about that time, on the inside of me—in my spirit—I heard these words: "Did you notice in the eleventh chapter of Mark and the twenty-third verse that the word 'say' in some form is in that verse *three* times and the word 'believe' is only there *once*?"

You see, God doesn't speak to your mind, and He doesn't speak to your body. God is a Spirit; He contacts you through your spirit. And you contact God with your spirit. It's easy enough to get quiet with your body. You lie down at night to go to sleep, and your body gets quiet. But your mind can sometimes go on and on.

But in this case, I had gotten both my body and my mind quiet, and the moment I did, that's when the Lord spoke to me. On the inside of me, in my spirit, I plainly heard the Lord speak. Now it wasn't like someone's voice speaking out loud that you can hear with your ears. I didn't hear it with my physical ears.

But yet way down on the inside—it was just as real as someone speaking to me physically—I heard those words. And when I did, I remember I rose up to a seated position and said out loud: "No. No, I didn't notice that!"

There's no telling how many thousands of times I'd quoted Mark 11:23 and 24. On the bed of sickness at the point of death, nearly all night long, I'd hang onto those verses. I'd say them over and over again. So there's no telling how many thousands of times I'd quoted these verses, but I'd never noticed that.

It's the same way with you. You may read certain chapters and verses for years, and then you'll be reading them one day and something just pops out from the page and you see something from the Word you've never seen before. You feel so silly and wonder why you never saw it before.

You see, you don't understand the Bible with your head. You've got to get the revelation of it in your heart. That's the reason you didn't see it before—because you didn't get it in your spirit.

So I said to the Lord: "No, I didn't notice that." Quickly, I turned the pages of my Bible back to Mark 11:23, and I read it.

MARK 11:23
23 For verily I say unto you, That whosoever shall SAY unto this mountain, Be thou removed, and be thou cast into the sea; and shall not doubt in his heart, but shall BELIEVE that those things which he SAITH shall come to pass; he shall have whatsoever he SAITH.

And there it was. I saw it. The word "say" in some form was in that verse three times, and "believe" was there only once.

I said to the Lord, "That's right! I never noticed that before, but that's right!"

And then on the inside of me I heard these words: "My people are not missing it primarily in their *believing*. But where they're missing it is in their *saying*. They have been taught to believe, but *faith must be released in words through your mouth*. You can have what you say."

Just Believing Is Not Enough

After He said that to me, I sat there on the floor before that altar and began to think back in my own life at every meeting and convention I'd ever attended.

All the ministers I'd ever heard preach flashed before my mind. And I couldn't remember a single one who ever preached about the "saying" part of faith.

Then Jesus went on to say to me in my spirit: "You're going to have to do three times as much preaching and teaching about the 'saying' part as you do the 'believing' part to get folks to see it."

And I checked up on myself. I had been doing a little bit of teaching on the saying part of faith, but not much along that line. But after that, I began to do what Jesus said to do. I preached and taught more about the saying part of faith.

Let's look at Mark 11:23 again and examine it. Notice, it says, *"and shall not doubt in his heart, but shall believe that those things which he saith."* In other words, that's saying, "but shall believe in his *heart* that those things which he *saith*." Those things which you *saith* are *words*.

In other words, you believe in your heart that those things—those *words*—which you saith shall come to pass. You believe in your heart, and you believe in your words. And that gives you power over demons, disease, and circumstances. Praise God forevermore!

Jesus concluded this verse by saying, *"he shall have whatsoever he saith."* What did Jesus say you were going to have? What you believed for? No. You see, a lot of people think, *Now if I believe strongly enough for something, it's going to come to pass.* But then they keep talking unbelief all the time.

You'll Have in Life What You Say

But, no. What you believe God for strongly won't necessarily come to pass just because you're believing strongly. Jesus didn't say, "He'll have whatsoever he believeth." Jesus said, *"he shall have whatsoever he SAITH."* He said you'll have what you say.

If you're not satisfied with what you've got, check up on what you're saying. Because all that you have, and all you are today, is the result of what you believed and said yesterday. Let that soak in!

There's a verse in the Old Testament that goes well along this line.

PROVERBS 6:2
2 Thou art snared with the words of thy mouth, thou art taken with the words of thy mouth.

A lot of Christians blame things on the devil when, really, they've been taken captive by the words of their own mouth. They are snared with the words of their mouth.

One writer put it this way: "You said you could not, and the moment you said it, you were whipped. You said you did not have faith, and doubt rose up like a giant and bound you. You were imprisoned with your own words. You talked failure, and failure held you in bondage."

Friends, mighty few of us realize that our words dominate us, and that's what Jesus is saying here in Mark 11:23: *"he shall have whatsoever he SAITH."*

Never talk failure. Never talk defeat. Never for one moment acknowledge that God's ability or power cannot put you over. If you're talking failure and defeat with your lips, you're acknowledging that God can't and hasn't put you over.

Instead of being failure-conscious, become God-conscious. Become God-inside minded. Remember, the Bible says in First John 4:4, *"Greater is he that is in you, than he that is in the world."*

I believe the Greater One is in me. I believe He's greater than the devil. I believe He's greater than the tests and trials I may face.

I believe He's greater than the storm I may be facing. I believe He's greater than the problems that may be confronting me. I believe He's greater than the circumstances that seem to have me bound. I believe He's greater than sickness and disease.

I believe He's greater than *anything* and *everything.* And He dwells in *me*! Hallelujah!

Very often I ask folks, "What's the Greater One doing in you? Is He just a spiritual hitchhiker? Did He just hitchhike a ride with you through life? Is He just extra baggage for you to carry?"

No! He's in there to help you. He's in there to strengthen you. He's in there to comfort you. Praise God, He's in there to put you over!

Friends, learn to use words that'll work for you. Your positive confession of God's Word will put you over in life. Jesus said you can have what you say.

You remember where it says in the Bible that when Israel came out of Egypt, they came right up to the border of Canaan's land to a place called Kadesh Barnea. And they sent twelve spies in to spy out the land, and ten of those spies brought back an evil report. Only two of them brought back a good report.

Don't Have an Evil Report

Now there's something here we need to see. What is an evil report? It's a report of *doubt.*

You know, a lot of Christians have an evil report. There's no use discussing what's more evil or less evil. If it's evil, we don't have any business with it.

A believer doesn't have any more business peddling doubt than he does peddling dope. Both doubt and dope are of the enemy. It's easy to excuse yourself for doubting, but that's the truth nonetheless.

Some folks think this is extreme, but I tell them that if I was pastoring, I'd rather have drug peddlers and bootleggers in my church than doubt peddlers!

Let me explain. You see, if you've got bootleggers and drug peddlers in your church, if you couldn't get them right with God, you could turn them out and everybody would be in favor of it. But you try to deal with some of these doubt peddlers and see what you get into!

They'll go around from house to house peddling doubt. They'll say, "See, the church is not going over. I told you it wouldn't. Sunday school's down, the money's down, and nothing's coming in.

That preacher's just leading us wrong, and he's even got the wrong evangelist to come here and preach."

These doubt peddlers look around for anybody they can find who's got a slop bucket for an ear so they can put a little slop in it!

No sir! The believer's got no business peddling doubt! Ten of those spies in the Book of Numbers brought back an evil report. The Bible said it was evil (Num. 13:32). What was the evil report? It was a report of doubt.

You see, God had already told them that the land they were going to was a land flowing with milk and honey. They brought back some of the giant clusters of grapes and the fruit of the land, and they said, "It is a land flowing with milk and honey, all right, *but . . .*"

People come to me for help sometimes, and I tell them, "Well, the Word of God says this. . . ," and I give them scriptures that answer their case. I've had them say to me, "Yes, I know that Brother Hagin, but you can't ever tell what might happen."

"Why, sure I can," I tell them. "Everything will happen that God said will happen if you'll believe it."

And so the Israelites brought back an evil report. They said, "*But,* there are giants in the land." The giants were there, all right. Sure they were. But the Israelites said, "In our own eyes we are grasshoppers. And we're grasshoppers in their sight too. We are not able to take the land" (Num. 13:33).

That was their confession. They confessed what they believed, and they believed they couldn't do it. They said, "We can't do it," and they got exactly what they said! Jesus said you can have what you say.

Caleb and Joshua brought back a *good* report. What did they say?

NUMBERS 13:30
30 And Caleb stilled the people before Moses, and said, Let us go up at once, and possess it; FOR WE ARE WELL ABLE TO OVERCOME IT.

The 10 spies had said, "We can't take the land." And they got exactly what they said. Israel accepted the majority report, and they said, "We can't take the land." They got exactly what they said. They couldn't take the land. They wandered in the wilderness and died—every one of the men from 20 years of age and upward, except Caleb and Joshua.

But Caleb said, *"LET US GO UP AT ONCE, and POSSESS it; for WE ARE WELL ABLE TO OVERCOME IT"* (Num. 13:30)!

Notice, Caleb didn't deny that the giants were there. And when we are faced with giants in our lives, we don't just stick our heads in the sand like an ostrich and think the giants will go away. No, they're there. But, blessed be God, we're well able to overcome them!

Now notice what Joshua said to the children of Israel about the giants in Canaan's land.

NUMBERS 14:9
9 Only rebel not ye against the Lord, neither fear ye the people of the land [yeah, the giants are there, but don't be afraid of them]; for THEY ARE BREAD FOR US: their defence is departed from them, and the Lord is with us: fear them not.

Put together what Caleb and Joshua said. They said, "We are *well* able to overcome. The Lord is with us!"

What does that mean to us today? When you're facing the giants of life, don't have a negative confession. Don't talk doubt and have an evil report. *Faith always has a good report.*

"Yeah," someone said. "But I can't do this and I can't do that."

Quit talking about what you can or can't do and talk about what the Greater One can do. Say, "I am well able to overcome the giants and take the land, for the Lord is with me. Greater is He Who is in me than he who is in the world. Jesus said, *'I will never leave thee, nor forsake thee'* (Heb. 13:5). God is with me now."

Once after a service, a woman came to me, and after sitting in the service and hearing faith and truth taught, she took hold of my hand and cried almost hysterically. (I'm not saying this to make fun of her. I'm just pointing out the facts.)

I said, "What's the matter, Sister?"

"Oh, I want you to pray for me."

"All right," I said, "what is it?"

"Well," she said, "it just seems like the Lord has forsaken me."

I said, "What awful sin have you committed to make Him forsake you?"

"Oh, Brother Hagin, as far as I know, I haven't done one thing wrong. But it just seems like the Presence of the Lord has gone from me."

I said, "Now where did you ever read in the Bible where it said, 'We walk by what things *seem like*'? The Bible didn't say we walk by what things seem like. It says we walk by *faith*. And Jesus said He'd never leave you or forsake you."

"I know that. But it just seems *like* He has."

"Well," I said, "you've got more faith in '*seems like*' than you have in the Bible."

"Yes, but I know what I *feel*." This woman almost got mad at me.

I answered her, "Yes, and I know my Jesus, and I'm not concerned about what I feel. If Jesus said it, I believe it."

Thank God for a motto I inherited from the Southern Baptists. I wrote it in red ink on the fly leaf in the Bible I had when I was on my deathbed. It says, "The Bible says it, I believe it, and that settles it."

That means I believe what the Word says whether things seem like the Bible is so or not—feeling or no feeling. And if you'll practice that and start *believing* right, thinking right, and *talking* right, it won't be long until you'll be *feeling* right too. Faith must be released. In other words, you can have what you say. Your faith can move mountains for you.

Chapter Six

Faith by Saying for Finances

For verily I say unto you, That whosoever shall say unto this mountain, Be thou removed, and be thou cast into the sea; and shall not doubt in his heart, but shall believe that those things which he saith shall come to pass; he shall have whatsoever he saith.

—Mark 11:23

We talked about the *"saying"* part of faith in Mark 11:23. But now I want to distinguish between *saying* and *praying*.

For instance, notice that the word "pray" is not mentioned in Mark 11:23. But the word "say" is mentioned.

Now let's read Mark 11:24.

MARK 11:24
24 Therefore I say unto you, What things soever ye desire, when ye PRAY, believe that ye receive them, and ye shall have them.

The sixth point to this study of faith is this: Faith will work by *saying* without *praying*.

Mark 11:23 never said a word about praying or prayer. Certainly, faith works in prayer. But when you *pray* it, you still have to *say* it.

Let's look at Mark 11:23 more closely. In this verse we can see faith working, without praying, by simply saying what you believe.

Jesus said, *"Whosoever shall say . . . and shall not doubt in his heart, but shall believe that those things which he saith shall come to pass; he shall have whatsoever he saith."*

Notice in this verse Jesus didn't say he'll have whatsoever he *prayeth.* He said he'll have whatsoever he *saith.*

Now these two verses, Mark 11:23 and 24, are the two verses of scripture that brought me off of the bed of sickness more than fifty-five years ago. These verses brought healing to my body from an almost total paralyzed condition, an incurable blood disease, and two serious organic heart troubles. Therefore, I've always been a stickler for these scriptures. And, of course, they're true because Jesus told the truth.

Actually, I was healed by a combination of both of these verses. As I said, when you pray, you still have to *say.* And it was on the bed of sickness after I'd *prayed* that I *said,* "I believe I receive healing." I said it out loud. I began to say *out loud,* not *think,* that I believed I received healing, and it was then that I began to amend, and every symptom disappeared.

Jesus didn't say, "Whosoever shall *think,* he shall have whatsoever he *thinketh.*" He said, *"Whosoever shall SAY . . . he shall have whatsoever he SAITH."*

I began to say out loud on my bed, "I believe I receive healing for my body," and I specified the things I was believing. I said, "I believe I receive healing of the heart condition, the paralysis, and the blood disease." And then, finally, in case I missed something, I just said, "I believe I receive healing from the top of my head to the soles of my feet."

That's what I believed, and that's what I said. Jesus said you'll have whatsoever you say. And when I began to say it, within the hour, every symptom of physical deficiency had disappeared, and I was standing out of bed on the floor completely healed.

Now don't misunderstand me. All manifestations of healing will not always come that fast. There's another scripture in the Bible that says, *"let us hold fast our profession* [or confession]" (Heb. 4:14). That's not talking about the confessing of sin. That's talking about holding fast to your confession of *faith*, because once you confess your sin, you're supposed to forget it because God forgets it (Heb. 8:12; 10:17).

When you confess your sin and repent, God said He forgave you and forgot it. So why would you want to remember it and confess it to Him again? God said, *"I, even I, am he that blotteth out thy transgressions for mine own sake, and will not remember thy sins"* (Isa. 43:25). Once you've repented and confessed your sin, He's forgotten it. And you should forget it too.

The confession that you're to hold fast to is the confession of your faith. I've held fast many a time on different things I'd confessed that I believed I received. Sometimes it was days before it came. And sometimes it was weeks before the answer came. And sometimes it was months before it came. And one time it was four years before it came. But it came! Praise God, I've never failed to receive.

With me personally, I've always just leaned more and stood more on Mark 11:23. I found it helpful to say it and not just pray it. I just said what I believed according to Mark 11:23.

I'm talking about the saying part of faith for something that concerns me, not the other person. When another person becomes involved, his will and what he believes has something to do with it. But in my own individual case, I've always leaned more and stood more on Mark 11:23. I've always just said it—I just said what I believed according to the Word.

Using Your Faith for Finances

Personally, I haven't prayed about money for years. And I've never been without it. I never pray about money. I just always say, "The money will come." And here it comes, praise God!

I remember on one occasion years ago, I needed $1,500 by the first of the month. So I said, "By the first of the month, I'll have $1,500."

I kept *saying* it at different times in prayer. I just said, "By the first of the month, I'll have $1,500." Well, when the first of the month came, I had $1,580. I had $80 more than I claimed!

The Lord actually taught me how to do that—how to use my faith for finances. For years, I hadn't seen it. I'd been saved and then healed by the power of God as a young Baptist boy. But I never thought about using my faith beyond salvation or healing.

Many people have gotten saved, but they've never thought about using their faith beyond believing God for salvation.

Even in prayer, they don't use their faith. There's always a struggle with them; they're always begging, crying, bawling, squalling, scratching, and pulling! And they get nothing; they stay defeated.

I don't know why, but early in my ministry, I went along for several years and never had anything, because I didn't believe for anything much financially or materially.

The last church I pastored was from 1946 over into 1949. My church was adequate—they took care of me. I think sometimes in situations like that, you don't have to do much believing. You just expect the church to take care of you.

But the Lord dealt with me, and I left my church and went out on the field. And I had a struggle the first year.

I went to the Lord in prayer about the situation. "Now, Lord," I said. "I did what You said to do." I mean, there wasn't even a shadow of a doubt about it. If I'd had a shadow of a doubt about going out on the field and leaving my church, I wouldn't even have waited on the doubt. I'd have taken advantage of the shadow and stayed put!

I didn't have a shadow of a doubt as to whether or not I was in the will of God. Somebody said, "Well, if you're in the perfect will of God and you're willing and obedient, everything's going to work just right, and He'll meet every need."

But you've still got to believe. If you don't believe, even though you're in the perfect will of God, it still won't work right. You've got to *appropriate* what belongs to you.

Some folks think these things will just fall on you automatically like ripe cherries off a tree. But they won't. The Bible says, "But without faith it is impossible to please him: for he that cometh to God must believe that he is, and that he is a rewarder of them that diligently seek him" (Heb. 11:6). God is a faith God. Faith has something to do with whether or not you receive the blessings of God.

I had all my figures in front of me, and I just brought them to the Lord in prayer. I said, "Here they are. Here's my gross income for this past year. If I'd stayed with my church (and they'd wanted me to stay), I would have had $1,200 more.

"Plus, besides getting $1,200 less, I've had to pay my own rent for my family while I was traveling. Before, I'd had the parsonage furnished, including all utilities paid. Plus we had much more to eat before, because a lot of folks would bring us something every time they came to church."

Sometimes we'd go visiting and come back and find the ice box full of food. The people in that church were very nice. About half of what we ate was furnished.

I continued talking to the Lord: "Now then, You said, *'If ye be willing and obedient, ye shall eat the good of the land'* (Isa. 1:19). I'm sure not eating the good. And I'm not wearing the good either. If You want us to *eat* the good, I know You want us to *wear* the good too. And if You want us to eat the good of the land, doesn't that mean You'll prosper us?"

I added: "If You want us to *eat* the good and *wear* the good, I know You want us to *drive* the good. I've never had a new car in my life. And the only car I had this year, I wore out. I just absolutely ran it ragged."

I didn't even have a spare tire, and the four tires that were on the car were baldies. The car was in such ill repair that I just sold it for junk. I didn't even get enough out of it to pay up what I owed. I had three notes, and I got enough money out of the car to pay the interest on the notes to renew them. I paid nothing on the principle. Then I had enough to buy the kids a few school clothes.

I said to the Lord: "My children are not adequately clothed or fed. But You said, *'If ye be willing and obedient, ye shall eat the good of the land.'"*

'Practice What You Preach'

I fasted and prayed about that for three days. And on the third day the Lord spoke to me and said, "The trouble with you is that you don't practice what you preach."

I held my stomach and said, "Lord, You've hit me a low blow." I came to my defense, as most of us would, and I said, "Lord, I *do* practice what I preach."

He said, "The trouble with you is, you *preach* faith but you don't *practice* faith."

"Why, Lord," I said, "I *do* practice faith. All these years after I got my healing as a young Baptist boy, I've always received healing.

Actually, I've never really been sick. I either get healed or begin to amend immediately. And I'm raising my children up that way, and they always receive healing."

All our children ever cost us, medically speaking, was $37.50. You see, when Ken was born, the doctor charged $25. That was the total price—he didn't give me a cut. (That's hard for some folks to realize because it costs a little more now!)

And then when our daughter, Pat, was born, the doctor charged $12.50. I was pastoring a different church when she was born, and the doctor there gave all pastors a fifty-percent discount.

Now don't misunderstand me. When the children got old enough to start school, we always took them to the doctor to have them examined.

But there was never anything wrong with them, and the doctor didn't charge us anything. He gave them the shots they needed to start school, but there wasn't anything wrong with them.

I remember when Ken was 12 years old he had the mumps for 45 minutes. We prayed, and they left him. He went right on to school the next day. You see, a lot of times, we just believe things have to be like they are, but they don't have to be that way.

So we raised our children to walk in divine health. I used my faith to believe for their healing while those children were young, but when they got older, they had to believe God for themselves. I couldn't carry them any longer.

I brought up that fact to the Lord. "Oh, yes," He said. "Sure, you practice faith when it comes to healing, and that's commendable. But that's as far as you ever went with your faith."

The Lord said to me: "Faith is the same in every realm and in every sphere. Now, you only use faith as far as salvation, the baptism of the Holy Ghost, and healing are concerned. But faith is the same in the financial realm."

The Lord continued: "Now then, if it were healing that you needed for your own body, you'd just claim that by faith, go out and publicly announce that you're healed, and go right on preaching. And many times in the past, every symptom would disappear while you were preaching.

"You've got to do the same thing when it comes to finances."

"Well, all right, Lord," I said. "I'll do that."

You Must Be Willing *and* Obedient

Then the Lord said, "But there is a matter here that's keeping it from working for you. Do you see that text you quoted to Me, 'If ye be willing and obedient, ye shall eat the good of the land'?"

Sometimes we glibly bring God's Word to Him, and He'll sure keep His Word if we measure up to it.

"Yes, Sir," I said. "That's right."

"Well," He said, "that scripture said, 'If ye be willing and obedient.' Now you've been obedient. You always talk about the fact that you're obeying Me. But, you know, you just never have been fully *willing.*"

I want to tell you, I got willing in 10 seconds! Don't tell me it takes a long time to become willing, because I know better.

I just made a little adjustment down on the inside, and I was *willing!* I'll tell you why it takes so long with some folks—it's that they're hard-headed and stubborn.

After I made the adjustment to become both willing and obedient, I said to the Lord: "Now I'm willing. I've been obedient all the time, because You already told me that I have. But now I'm willing, so I fill the bill. Praise God, now I'm ready to eat the good of the land."

The Lord said, "I know you're willing. Now then, I'll tell you what to do. "First, don't ever pray about money, that is, in the sense that you have been praying about it."

The Lord wasn't telling me not to pray. He was just telling me not to pray about money the way I had been praying. Prayer is a subject that's misunderstood by a lot of folks.

For example, somebody said that praise is the highest type of prayer, because prayer is really fellowshipping with God. So when you're praising God, you're praying in the highest sense. That's true.

But a lot of times what we call prayer isn't prayer. So many times we think of prayer only as asking God for something. You've heard the saying, "My name is Jimmy; I'll take all You'll gimme."

Or we're like the old farmer who always prayed, "God bless me and my wife and my son John and his wife—us four and no more." And we think that's prayer. But if we're praying that way, all we're doing is mouthing words.

The Lord had told me, "Don't ever pray about money anymore in the way you've been praying about it."

I asked Him, "Then what am I going to do?"

He said, "The money you need is down there; it's not up here in Heaven. I'm not going to rain any money down from Heaven, because if any money came raining down from up here, it would be counterfeit, and I'm not a counterfeiter.

"You see, I put everything you need in the earth. I made it all, and I didn't make it for the devil and his crowd."

So many times people think, "You know, you ought not to have anything if you're living for God. If you're a Christian, you ought to go through life with the soles of your shoes, the top of your hat, and the seat of your britches worn out, living on Barely-Get-Along Street way down at the end of the block right next to Grumble Alley." And that's supposed to be a sign of humility.

No, it isn't. It isn't a sign of humility. It's a sign of ignorance of the Word.

God said to me: "You read in My Word, in Psalm 50:10–12, where it says, *'every beast of the forest is mine, and the cattle upon a thousand hills . . . the world is mine, and the fulness thereof.'* And in Haggai 2:8 it says, *'The silver is mine, and the gold is mine.'*

"It's Mine because I created it. And I didn't make it for Myself. I made it for My man Adam. And I said, 'Adam, I give you dominion over *all* the work of My hands'" (Gen. 1:26, 28).

The Lord continued: "Originally, Adam was to dominate this world. He had dominion over the cattle of a thousand hills. He had dominion over the silver and the gold. And he had dominion over the world and the fullness thereof. But Adam committed high treason— he became a traitor—and sold out to Satan. And Satan became the god of this world."

Second Corinthians 4:4 calls Satan the god of this world. So Satan is dominating the world because Adam gave him the permission to do it by committing high treason.

Since Satan is dominating the world, he's dominating the silver and the gold and the cattle of a thousand hills too.

But Jesus came to redeem us from the hand of the enemy, hallelujah! And in the Name of Jesus we have the authority to claim the money we need.

The Lord said to me: "Whatever you need, claim it in Jesus' Name. You say, 'Satan, take your hands off my money,' because it's Satan that's keeping it from coming—not Me.

"It's not Me keeping your children from being fed adequately. It's not Me keeping your children from being clothed adequately."

And I saw it! I got the light on it, praise God. I remember when I first put into practice what the Lord had shown me, I did it with fear and trembling.

When I received this revelation, I was holding a meeting in a little church down in east Texas. I had preached there the year before and they had paid me $57.15 a week for two weeks. They had given me a total of $114.30 for two weeks.

This was more than fifty years ago. I knew that if they thought they had adequately paid me at $57 a week, it would have to be God for me to get what I needed to meet my budget. (There was just a small group of them, and they thought $50 a week was just fine. They thought that was big pay for any preacher.)

So I said, "All right, Lord. I'll just prove that out here at this church. I'm claiming $150 this week."

Now I knew that if you suggested to this church that they pay even $75, they'd all fall over backwards. And if you had suggested a $100, they'd say, "Well, that would take a miracle." And if you had said $150, they'd say, "God Himself couldn't do that!" In other words, that would have been beyond their wildest imagination.

And I knew if I told the pastor what I was believing for, it would have scared him. So I said to him: "During the meeting, don't put any pressure on folks for money. Don't say, 'Who'll give this or that.'" Sometimes in the past, the pastor would spend a long time on the offering if the church was running short on finances.

I told him, "Just pass the plate, that's all. Just give people a chance to give."

And so I held fast to my confession and said, "Satan, take your hands off my money." And after I'd been in that meeting a few days, the pastor asked me to stay another week. The Lord told me to stay ten days total, so I changed what I'd claimed and said, "Now, Lord, in Jesus' Name, I'm claiming $200 for the ten days."

When it was all over, the pastor handed me my offering, and it came to $240.15. The pastor said, "Man, that's the most we've ever done. I don't understand it. I just can't figure it out."

I went to another church. It wasn't a large church at all. They only ran about 90 in Sunday school, but a few more than that attended the night services.

And I said to this pastor, "Now be sure not to put any pressure on the people for money. Just pass the plate and give them a chance to give."

And so the very first week I was at this church, after all the money was in, he gave it to me and said, "You know Brother Hagin, we've never paid anybody this much money. Do you know how much money came in for you this week? Here's more than $280.

"We average about $90 a week," the pastor continued. "We had one minister come preach who was in a bind financially because of some bills he had to pay. I got up in front of the congregation, and it took me forty-five minutes of asking the people to finally get him $140 for one week. And here I haven't said a word, and you got more than $280. I just don't understand it."

"That's all right, Brother," I said. "I understand it thoroughly."

I had some of the most unusual experiences back then in the area of finances that you've ever seen. And I experienced God's blessing in some of the most unlikely places, because God's Word works!

Hold Fast to That Which Is Good

I like to do some things just to prove out what I learn from God and His Word. The Bible said, *"Prove all things; hold fast that which is good"* (1 Thess. 5:21).

For example, when I got a hold of this truth about finances, I had to prove it in my own life first. And you talk about scraping the bottom of the barrel. I wasn't just scraping the bottom of the barrel—I was *under* the barrel, and the barrel was on top of me! But I got out, praise God, and started rising to the top. And I've been rising to the top ever since!

After the Lord taught me about prosperity back there in that church and showed me how to get my needs met, then I began to see some things about the saying part of faith.

I went home from that meeting and said to my wife: "Honey, here we are living in a little three-room apartment. We need a bigger place to live."

My father-in-law had passed away. He'd lived his life out and had gone on to be with Jesus. And my mother-in-law was staying with us part time and with her son some of the time too.

So I said to Oretha, "Let's just get us a house."

"Well," she said, "can we afford it?" I began to tell her what the Lord said to me.

She said, "Yes, we can afford it. God will do that for us."

So we rented a three-bedroom home. After we had moved into this house, I said to Oretha, "You know, we could buy this house and our payment would be less than what we're paying for rent. At least we'd be building up a little equity."

So we claimed that. I got out and walked around the yard. The Bible said, *"Every place that the sole of your foot shall tread upon, that have I given unto you"* (Josh. 1:3).

At that time, I was gone 90 percent of the time traveling in the field. In fact, sometimes I'd preach 50 or 51 weeks out of 52. I'd preach, take off Christmas week, and start again on the road the next Sunday.

I said to my wife, "Now you go talk to the landlord and see what she wants for the house." We were just acting like she wanted to sell it!

So my wife wrote back (we wrote each other a letter every day). In her letter, Oretha said, "The landlord said she didn't want to sell the house." Her husband had built the house himself and had put some extras into it. They moved away because of his job but were planning to move back there.

I didn't let that daunt me. I wrote back to Oretha and said, "She wants to sell it; she just doesn't know it yet!" We just acted like the house was ours, and in every letter we talked like it was ours.

Then in two or three months, I wrote and said to my wife, "Go ask the landlord again." Oretha asked again, and she wrote back and said, "No, she said they weren't going to sell." I wrote back and said, "Yes, she is; she just doesn't know it."

I said to my wife, "I'm going to be holding a meeting close to home. This would be a good time for us to get together with the landlord. I can drive over in the afternoon after my morning service, and we can all discuss it.

So Oretha went to see the landlord again. She called me and said, "I asked her to set up a meeting on a certain day, and she said they still weren't interested."

I said, "Well, don't let that bother you, because they are interested; they just don't know it yet."

The very next day my wife called me and said, "Honey, I've got good news. The landlord just called me and said they have decided to sell the house."

I said, "Why, I've been knowing that for nearly a year."

Oretha said, "I've set up the meeting for tomorrow afternoon at 2:30."

I said, "All right. After my morning service I'll come home, and we'll have lunch together. Then we'll meet with them."

We met with them, and to make a long story short, we got the house. Somebody else had been wanting the house, too, and he offered them an awfully good price—more than we offered them. Actually, what he offered them was more than the house was really worth. I think that was one reason they decided to sell it.

We kept bargaining with them until we were only $500 away from the other folks' price. That was a lot of money in those days.

I needed to get back to the church for my night meeting, so finally, I said, "I sure would hate for you folks to miss God." They were Christians, but they weren't Spirit-filled Christians. However, later that same year, they were filled with the Spirit.

The woman began to laugh, and she said to her husband, "Honey, tell them what you told me."

He said, "No, you go ahead and tell them."

"Well," she said, "we're Christians, and we pray together every night before we go to bed.

"The last three nights after we've prayed, my husband said to me, 'Honey, something on the inside of me tells me that the house belongs to that preacher and his wife.'"

I said, "See, that's what I'm talking about. I'd sure hate for you to miss God."

They said, "You can buy the house. It's yours."

That's the same way we got our second house, our third house, and our fourth house. We just said it according to Mark 11:23. And it never involved a dime of our own money.

That's also the way we got our first new automobile. I told every pastor I held a meeting for, "I'm going to buy a new car in the fall when the new cars come out."

"What are you going to buy?"

Well, I knew if God wanted us to eat the good of the land, He wanted us to drive the best. So I said, "I'm going to buy the best there is."

I was in a particular meeting one fall. It was about the same time we got the house I was telling you about. When I first walked in the parsonage door, I said to the pastor and his wife, "I'm going to buy a new car while I'm here. I hope it doesn't hurt my offerings."

Some folks, bless their hearts, if they ever pray for the preacher, they pray: "Lord, you keep him humble, and we'll keep him poor." And they think they're doing God a favor!

The pastor said, "Oh, no. It won't affect my church. In fact, we'll help you buy it. What kind are you going to buy?" I told him the kind of car I was interested in.

He said, "Well, I tell you what—one of the deacons in my church has a brother who's in the car business. He handles that particular make.

"In fact, I stopped by there to see him myself day before yesterday, and they were unloading one off the truck.

"I looked at it, and it's got all the equipment you want."

I said, "It sounds like just the one I want."

I didn't think any more about it. A day or two after we started the meeting, the pastor said to me, "Come, get in the car and go with me." So we drove to this car dealership.

He said, "There's the car I was telling you about." I looked at it and said, "I'd forgotten to tell you the color, but that's the exact color I had in mind."

In this illustration, this is the point I want to show you: Not only will faith work by saying it, but faith will work in your heart with doubt in your head. Many times because people have a doubt in their minds, they think, "Well, my faith won't work. I'm doubting."

But every time I would tell a preacher, "I'm going to buy a new car in the fall," my head would say, "Where are you going to get the money? You couldn't even buy an old sitting hen!"

When that pastor and I drove to that dealership and saw that car sitting there, I was having trouble with my head the whole time. My head said, "You've got enough sense to know better than to lie. Here you've talked in front of this pastor about how you're going to buy a car, and he's about to find out what a fraud you are.

"You've talked faith and preached faith, and you're going to fall flat on your face because you can't buy that car. You don't have any money. (And I didn't!) And all you've got is an old car that's got 93,000 miles on it. And it needs a valve job, and the transmission is leaking. You don't even have a spare, and all your tires are bald.

"You can't get anything for that old car. You ought to sell it for junk. You can't get enough out of it to make a down-payment on that new car. You can't, and you know you can't. You can't buy that car."

I just didn't pay any attention to my head or the devil either. We looked the car over and went inside the office. A fellow with a big black cigar in his mouth was sitting there talking on the phone. He had his feet propped up on his desk.

He finished his conversation, put down his cigar, and stood up to greet us. The pastor introduced me as his evangelist who was in town for a meeting. We all sat down, and the man picked up his cigar and began to smoke. He propped his feet up on his desk again (it was his desk—he could do whatever he wanted to!).

The pastor said to the man, "Brother Hagin wants that car right out there."

The man looked out the window at the car and said, "Well, fine, Reverend." And he put his cigar down and became very serious. He said, "I may be just a sinner, but there's one thing I believe. I believe the man of God ought to have the best in life."

You know, sometimes an old sinner's got better principles about these things than some saints—or "ain'ts"!

The car dealer said, "Reverend, do you know how much that car is worth?"

"Yes," I said, "I know." The new models had been out about three weeks, and I'd been checking the prices, but I'd never found a color I wanted. I quoted him the price.

He said, "That's exactly right. That's what the retail price is. Do you know what I paid for the car?"

He opened his desk drawer and handed me a piece of paper. He had paid about $1,200 less than the list price.

He said, "What you see there is exactly what it cost me. And I'm going to let you have it for that. I'm not going to make a penny on it. I'm going to let you have it for just exactly what it cost me."

He asked, "Do you want to trade anything in on it?"

"Well," I said, "I don't have any money. I'll just have to trade my old car in on it."

"All right," he said, "what do you have?"

I said, "I'll just be honest with you," and I told him my car was several years old. I said, "I've put 93,000 miles on it myself. I don't know how much somebody else may have put on it, because I got it used. The transmission is leaking. It needs a valve job—it clatters like a Model-T Ford hitting on two cylinders. It just jumps and jerks."

I continued: "I don't even have a spare tire, and all four tires on the car are baldies. The car is not worth much."

"Reverend," he said, "do you know what cars like yours are selling for?"

I said, "Yes, I've checked them on the lot. Good, clean ones that are in top-notch condition sell for anywhere from $795 to $995."

He said, "Yours is probably worth about $495."

I said, "I doubt that. I wouldn't give $495 for it."

He said, "This is what I'm going to do. I'm going to allow you $995 for your car as a trade-in on this new one. As I said, I'm not making a penny on it, and I'll lose money on your old one. I'll put yours back there in the garage and do the valve job, fix the transmission, put tires on it, and clean it up. And I still won't get that much out of it. I'll probably have to sell it for $795 at the most.

"It'll cost me probably two or three hundred dollars to make this deal. But sign this contract, and you can drive that new car off the lot today."

And I drove it home! And do you know that from that day to this, I've never been without a new car. I found out how to get one, praise God! God's Word works!

God taught me these principles of mountain-moving faith for finances. I remember years ago we were traveling with some friends, and I just suddenly said to them, "Somebody's going to give Kenneth Hagin Ministries $10,000." We wanted to pay off our office building in Tulsa. Now I said that in faith on the basis of what Jesus said to me from the Word: "You can have what you say." And it wasn't three months till an Episcopal woman gave us a check for $10,000, and we paid off our building.

I never asked anybody for anything. God's Word works!

And then on another occasion after I got the $10,000 check, because you can have what you say, I turned to my office force and said, "All of you, listen to me right now: Somebody's going to give us $25,000."

And somebody did! You can have what you say.

Somebody said, "What did you do with the money?"

I didn't take a penny of it. I used it all for God and His work.

I'm going to get on *more* radio stations. I'm going to publish *more* books. I'm going to make *more* tapes. I'm going to get the truth out to folks. Somebody else is going to get blessed by it, praise God! I'm not going to take one nickel of it, not one single dime, any more than I did the $10,000 or the $25,000.

Prosperity Is God's Will

Somebody else said, "Well, I just don't like that prosperity business." I said, "Neither does the devil, but I'm not going to pay any attention to you or the devil either."

"Yeah," he said, "but I'm just against all that." I said, "So were Hitler, Mussolini, and Stalin. I'm not going to listen to any of the four of you!"

I'm in favor of prosperity, and so is God. He said, *"If ye be willing and obedient, ye shall eat the good of the land"* (Isa. 1:19).

Third John 2 says, *"Beloved, I wish above all things that thou mayest prosper and be in health, even as thy soul prospereth."*

"Beloved, I wish above all things that thou mayest prosper." That's talking about financial prosperity.

The phrase, *"and be in health,"* is talking about physical prosperity. And the phrase, *"even as thy soul prospereth,"* is talking about spiritual prosperity.

Appropriating the Blessings of God

How does it all come about? By *saying*, by *saying*, by *saying*! *"For . . . whosoever shall SAY unto this mountain, Be thou removed, and be thou cast into the sea; and shall not doubt in his heart, but shall believe that those things which he SAITH shall come to pass; he shall have whatsoever he SAITH"* (Mark 11:23).

Faith works by saying without necessarily praying. But faith also works by praying. Mark 11:24 says, *"when ye PRAY, believe that ye receive them, and ye shall have them."*

MARK 11:23–24
23 For verily I say unto you, That whosoever shall say unto this mountain, Be thou removed, and be thou cast into the sea; and shall not doubt in his heart, but shall believe that those things which he saith shall come to pass; he shall have whatsoever he saith.
24 Therefore I say unto you, What things soever ye desire, when ye pray, believe that ye receive them, and ye shall have them.

Mark 11:23 talks about "*saying* it," and Mark 11:24 talks about "praying it." Read those two verses and underline this thought: *There is just a shade of difference in what you believe if you say it or if you pray it.* In other words, if you just say it, you believe that those things which you say shall come to pass. And if you just *pray* it, you believe that you receive when you pray and that you shall have whatever it is you desired and prayed for.

Too many times we say we believe, but then we leave it at that. But Jesus didn't say, "Just believe." Jesus tells you exactly what to believe: *"Whosoever shall say . . . and shall not doubt in his heart, but shall BELIEVE THAT THOSE THINGS WHICH HE SAITH SHALL COME TO PASS; he shall have whatsoever he saith."*

What does he believe? He believes that those things which he saith shall come to pass.

Now in the case of the house I was telling you about, my wife and I kept believing over a period of a year's time that what we said would come to pass. And it came to pass!

You see, in Mark 11:23, *"Whosoever shall say . . . and shall not doubt in his heart, but shall believe that those things which he saith shall come to pass,"* it hasn't come to pass yet. But he *believes* that those things which he saith shall come to pass. They haven't come to pass yet. If they'd already come to pass, he wouldn't have to believe it. If those things which he saith had already come to pass, he'd *know* it; he wouldn't have to *believe* it.

Bless so many people's darling hearts—they're walking by *sight!* Somebody said, "Well, I can't see it; therefore, I don't have it. I believe God's going to do it *sometime.*" And they miss the whole thing.

No, according to Mark 11:23, you're to keep believing that those things which you saith shall come to pass. In my own life, a lot of times,

I just keep saying right in the face of contradictory circumstances, "It shall come to pass." That's what Jesus told me to believe.

Jesus didn't tell me to believe I've got it. If I've got it, I can feel it and see it, and everybody else can feel it and see it too.

Oh, I know the crowd will look at you funny when you talk about faith—even other Christians—bless their hearts! They're walking by sight. People who do that are filled with doubt. And they'll look at you like you're a little bit off, but don't let it disturb you, because you know *they're* the ones who are off, and you're the one who's on—on God's Word! Hallelujah!

According to Mark 11:23, you're to believe that those things you say shall come to pass. And what will happen? Sooner or later, you shall have whatsoever you say.

I know what I'm talking about. I've been there. I put it to practice under all kinds of circumstances. And I know it's true because Jesus said it. He's not a liar.

Don't misunderstand me. That doesn't mean we're not going to have any tests or trials or that every blessing God has provided is just always going to fall on us like ripe cherries off a tree.

Back in the beginning of my Christian walk and ministry, I didn't understand faith like I understand it now. But I learned both from God's Word and from experiencing for myself that what His Word says is the absolute truth. And the Lord said to me, "Now you go teach My people what I've taught you."

Hold Fast to Your Confession of Faith

I've been there years ago when I've gotten into my car to go home after a meeting, and I counted my offering, and it wasn't enough. I was behind on my house rent. I owed this bill and that one. And I would start driving home at nighttime because my tires were thin and couldn't hold up under the daytime heat.

I would drive off, knowing I didn't have another meeting to hold, so I don't have any income. I was in the full-time ministry, and the Bible says, *"The Lord ordained that they which preach the gospel should live of the gospel"* (1 Cor. 9:14).

I'd drive at nighttime when it was cool. I had the car windows rolled down, and as I drove, it seemed like one of those tires picked up and began to sing a song: *What are you going to do now? What are you going to do now? What are you going to do now? What are you going to do now?*

And then one of the other tires joined in—they had a duet: *What are you going to do now? What are you going to do now? What are you going to do now?*

Then the third tire seemed to join in and start singing, *What are you going to do now? What are you going to now?*

And *finally*, there was a quartet—all four of them were singing, *What are you going to do now? What are you going to do now? What are you going to do now?*

So finally, I just yelled right out loud: "You know what I'm going to do? I'll tell you exactly what I'm going to do. I'm just going to act like the Bible is so. I'm going home, and I'm going to bed. I'm going to sleep like a baby, that's what I'm going to do!"

And I went home. My dear wife was concerned. She said, "How much money do we have? What was your offering?" You see, while I was traveling, she was at home with the bills.

I said, "Everything's fine, praise God. We don't have a care." I said that in faith because you can have what you say. "Everything's fine. Just go to sleep. We'll talk about it in the morning."

Oretha got up in the morning and got the kids off to school. I didn't get in until about three o'clock in the morning, so she let me sleep in. And I was still asleep in the morning until the phone rang and woke me up.

Oretha answered the phone, and I heard her say, "He got in late, and he's still asleep. I hate to disturb him."

I said, "What is it, Honey?"

"Somebody's calling long distance."

I said, "I'll take it." The phone had a long cord, so she just brought it to the bed.

The person on the other line said, "Brother Hagin, you don't know me, but I'm a pastor in ____" (and he named the town). "I was wondering, when could you start me a meeting?"

I said, "Tomorrow night." Glory to God!

You Can Have What You Say

Folks who don't live by faith have missed a lot. To make a long story short, everything worked out fine. I didn't lose a wink of sleep or miss a meal over my circumstances. And God met every need!

Faith works! When you believe that those things which you say shall come to pass, you shall have whatsoever you say!

Now, if you use your faith in prayer, what are you to believe? Look at Mark 11:24 and see: *"Therefore I say unto you, What things soever ye desire, WHEN YE PRAY, BELIEVE that ye receive them, and ye shall have them."* What things soever you desire *when you pray*—not after you pray, not next week, not next month—but at *that very moment* when you pray, *believe!*

What Do You Believe?

"Oh, Brother Hagin. I believe. I believe."

What do you believe?

"Well, I believe in prayer."

It's good that you believe in prayer, but in Mark 11:24, that's not what Jesus said to believe.

"Well, I believe the Bible's so." That's good, but that won't work here. In Mark 11:24, that's not what Jesus said to believe.

"Well, I believe in the Holy Ghost." That's wonderful. Praise the Lord, I do too. But believing in the Holy Ghost won't work here, because there are a lot of people who believe in the Holy Ghost who don't get their prayers answered.

"Well, I believe prayer changes things." That's wonderful too. It does. Prayer does change things. But just believing that won't work here.

No, Jesus tells us in Mark 11:24 exactly what to believe. He said that *when you pray*, believe you receive.

Here again is where people who walk by sight have trouble. They're not going to believe anything until they see it. They say, "When I see the money in my hand, then I'll believe."

Or, for instance, if it's healing they desire, they say, "When I *feel* like I'm healed and all the symptoms disappear, then I'll believe."

But if you waited till all the symptoms disappeared, you wouldn't have to believe you had received a thing then—you'd *know* it. For instance, I wouldn't have to *believe* I received a hundred dollar bill if I had a hundred dollar bill in my hand. If I had a hundred dollar bill in my hand, I'd *know* it.

But when you pray, believe that you'll have what things soever you desire. Begin to say that from your heart because you believe it. And if you don't believe it, start saying it anyhow, and you can school yourself into faith. "I believe that I receive. I believe that I receive." What will happen? The rest of that verse says, "*and ye shall have them.*"

You see, the *having* is going to come. But the having doesn't come first. The *believing* comes first and then the *having* comes. Most folks want it turned around; they want to have it first, then they'll believe it. But that wouldn't take any faith, and the Bible says, "The just shall live by faith" (Rom. 1:17).

In order to move mountains in your life, you need to believe according to God's Word, and you need to *speak* according to God's Word. You possess mountain-moving faith, and you can use your faith *by saying* for the financial prosperity the Lord has provided for you.

Using Mountain-Moving Faith for Others

And Jesus answering saith unto them, Have faith in God.

For verily I say unto you, That whosoever shall say unto this mountain, Be thou removed, and be thou cast into the sea; and shall not doubt in his heart, but shall believe that those things which he saith shall come to pass; he shall have whatsoever he saith.

Therefore I say unto you, What things soever ye desire, when ye pray, believe that ye receive them, and ye shall have them.

And when ye stand praying, forgive, if ye have ought against any: that your Father also which is in heaven may forgive you your trespasses.

But if ye do not forgive, neither will your Father which is in heaven forgive your trespasses.

—Mark 11:22–26

I've talked about six important facts of faith that will enable you to move mountains in your life. You can put your faith to work for yourself in your own life, and your faith will *always* work for you!

Now, sometimes, but not always, you can make your faith work for someone else.

I want to call your attention especially to Mark 11:24. Notice that the very first word of that verse is *"Therefore."* Somebody once said, "When you find a "therefore" in the Bible, stop right there and find out what it's *there for*!" That's a good suggestion.

That word, "therefore," joins what Jesus was about to say to what He'd just said.

In Mark 11:23, Jesus had just said, *"For verily I say unto you, That whosoever shall say unto this mountain, Be thou removed, and be thou cast into the sea; and shall not doubt in his heart, but shall BELIEVE that THOSE THINGS WHICH HE SAITH SHALL COME TO PASS; he shall have whatsoever he saith."*

In Mark 11:24, Jesus is saying, "Therefore, I say unto *you*, what things soever *yo*u desire when you pray, you believe you receive them, and you shall have them." Now, that verse means all of us in general, but it's speaking about you and your desires.

You see, you're not going to be able to push *your* desires off on somebody else. Jesus is talking in Mark 11:24 about you and your desires. So if what you desire is not somebody else's desire, you're not going to be able to push your desires off on them.

In the case where somebody else is involved in your praying, their will comes into play in the situation. You can pray for them and with them. But you'll have to get them to agree with you.

MATTHEW 18:19
19 Again I say unto you, That if two of you shall agree on earth as touching any thing that they shall ask, it shall be done for them of my Father which is in heaven.

The Bible says something else along this line.

AMOS 3:3
3 [How] Can two walk together, except they be agreed?

You're not going to get somebody healed by you believing they'll live while they believe they'll die! There's no agreement there.

I've had people to come to me and say, "Brother Hagin, I want you to pray with me."

"What for?" I'd ask them.

"Well, you use that scripture, Matthew 18:19, that says, *'If two of you shall agree on earth as touching any thing that they shall ask, it shall be done for them of my Father which is in heaven.'*"

"Yes," I'd say.

"Well, I want you to pray with me," and they'd tell me their prayer request.

As a usual thing I'll say, "All right. Let's just join hands right now and agree." And most of the time I'll say, "Listen while I pray, and you agree with it, because if we both pray at once and don't pay attention to each other, you may be praying in one direction and I may be praying in another direction.

"So you just listen to what I say and agree with it."

Hoping Is Not Believing

I'm thinking of one lady in particular. She asked me to pray with her about a financial need. I said, "Father, we agree concerning this $100 that this family needs by the first of next month. And we agree that by the first of the month they'll have this extra $100.

"Lord, You said, '*If two of you shall agree on earth as touching any thing that they shall ask, it shall be done for them of my Father which is in heaven.*' So now, because we agree that it's done, we thank You, Father, because it shall happen. And we thank You for it right now in the Name of Jesus. Amen."

The woman said, "Amen." Then I said, "Sister, is it done?" She tuned up and started bawling, saying, "Well, I sure hope so, Brother Hagin. I *hope* it is."

I said, "It isn't then. It isn't, because you're hoping and I'm believing. There's no agreement there. We didn't agree."

That's the reason many fail when they come forward to receive healing. Many fail because they're hoping, and we're believing. There's no agreement, so we don't make any faith connection.

Who Can You 'Carry' With Your Faith?

Then under what circumstances can you help others with your own faith? First of all, as long as people are genuine baby Christians, you can carry them with your faith. I know there are a lot of people who are baby Christians who shouldn't be baby Christians, and you can't carry those people. But you can carry folks on your faith as long as they are really genuine baby Christians — new Christians.

There is a likeness between physical growth and spiritual growth. You know, nobody's born a full-grown human. They're born babies, and they grow up.

In the same way, nobody is born a full-grown Christian either. They're born babies, and then they're supposed to grow up.

Peter said, *"As newborn babes desire the sincere milk of the word, that ye may grow thereby"* (1 Peter 2:2).

Paul wrote a letter to the Church at Ephesus and said, *"That we henceforth be no more children, tossed to and fro, and carried about with every wind of doctrine"* (Eph. 4:14).

Paul wasn't writing to a children's church. They had some adults in that church. The Book of Acts records that Paul went to Ephesus. He saw something was missing, and he said, *"Have ye received the Holy Ghost since ye believed?"* (Acts 19:2).

They said, *"We have not so much as heard whether there be any Holy Ghost."* Paul said unto them, *"Unto what then were ye baptized? And they said, Unto John's baptism"* (Acts 19:3).

ACTS 19:4-7

4 Then said Paul, John verily baptized with the baptism of repentance, saying unto the people, that they should believe on him which should come after him, that is, on Christ Jesus.
5 When they heard this, they were baptized in the name of the Lord Jesus.
6 And when Paul had laid his hands upon them, the Holy Ghost came on them; and they spake with tongues, and prophesied.
7 And all the MEN were about twelve.

Paul laid hands on them, and they received the Holy Ghost and spake with tongues and prophesied. And the number of the men was about twelve. So I know that church had twelve men in it. I don't know how many women and children there were, but it tells you the number of men who there were.

So there were people in that church who were grown folks physically, but they were still children spiritually. Paul was trying to get them to grow up.

As I said, there is a likeness between physical growth and spiritual growth. For example, when a baby is born in the natural, unless somebody cares for that baby and dresses and feeds it, it will die. It's similar with newborn Christians.

Newborn Christians Must Be Nurtured in the Faith

I remember I was holding a meeting for a fellow one time, bless his heart. He had a good church. I never could understand why he had as good a church as he did. But he did. And he'd just built a new auditorium that would seat about 800 people. He wrote me a letter, phoned me, and came to one of my meetings and talked to me personally about holding a meeting for him. Then he sent me a telegram, trying to get me to come and hold a meeting for him.

"Brother Hagin, I've just got a new auditorium finished that'll seat 800. It seats 600, plus we have room for 200 folding chairs. I'll guarantee you, the house will be full every night."

I went eventually. And it was just like he said. He didn't run 800. He ran 400 or 500 in attendance. But the church was full every night.

We had services every night, including Saturday night. I wasn't having day services at that time.

The pastor and I agreed to carry the meeting into a second week, and then on the Saturday night of the second week, we agreed to carry the meeting into a third week.

On that Saturday night when I gave the altar call for people to come to be saved and filled with the Spirit, 39 people came. Most of them had either been backslidden and were coming back to God, or they had never been saved before and were coming to God.

We had prayer rooms beside the platform, and they weren't very large. Thirty-nine people couldn't have gotten into one of them, so we put the ladies in one prayer room and the men in the other one. And we had a man lead the men's prayer room and a lady to lead the ladies' prayer room.

I noticed at the altar that there were seven young couples who came forward. I'd say they were anywhere from 28 to 32 years of age.

Afterward, I asked the pastor, "Did you know those seven young couples who came to the altar?" He didn't know a one of them. They were strangers—they had never been to his church before.

"Well," I said, "were they backsliders?"

"No," he said, "they were brand-new converts. They'd never been saved, and they'd never been a member of anybody's church." One or two of them never had even gone to church much in their entire lives. And they all got saved that night.

I said, "Did you get their names and addresses?" I didn't have any cards with me.

"No," he said, "I just figure if they got anything from God, they'll be back."

I said to him right then, "I'm closing the meeting tomorrow night," and I told him why. A fellow like that is not very smart. And I closed the meeting.

Somebody's going to have to see after the spiritual babies!

I pastored nearly 12 years, and I learned a few things in that length of time. I feel sorry for pastors, because the spiritual nurseries are full of old babies. I mean, if you got somebody saved, there would be no place to put them because nobody else is going to get up and give him his bed in the spiritual nursery!

And these older spiritual babies aren't going to give the newer babies their bottles either. If you take the bottle away from some of these older Christians who've been saved and filled with the Spirit for years, you'll have a cry on your hands!

Two Types of Spiritual Babies

I'll illustrate the difference between a genuine baby Christian and a spiritual baby who's been a Christian for years.

There was a fellow in the last church I pastored who was a businessman. He was a contractor by trade. His wife was one of my Sunday school teachers.

This man wasn't a Christian, but he never missed a service—Sunday school, Sunday morning, or Sunday night. And during revival meetings, he'd come every night and bring his family.

Finally, this man said to his wife, "Talk to Brother Hagin for me. I know I'm not saved, but ask Brother Hagin if the church would accept my tithes."

This man and another fellow were in business together. The other fellow belonged to another church; he wasn't a Christian either. This woman's husband told his business partner, "Our business is in bad shape financially. We're just about bankrupt. I know we're not Christians, but I believe if we'd honor God by paying our tithes that God would honor us."

Of course we accepted his tithes! And so he started bringing his tithes from his part of the business. Then he bought out his partner, and within 90 days' time, his business was out of the red and in the black, and it was prospering.

Then he needed to hire other folks to help him in his business. And so he'd hire people from the church to work for him.

Even before he got saved, this man said to me, "Before I hire anybody, I ask them on a questionnaire, 'Do you pay tithes?' My older employees who have been with me can stay with me. I wouldn't fire a man for not paying tithes. But I don't hire anybody who doesn't pay tithes. This is a tithe-paying organization. I've proved it out, and it works!"

That's a pretty good attitude for a sinner man.

But then this man came to the altar one night in a service and was gloriously saved. He continued to hire people from the church to work, including the young people for summertime help. I checked up on the finances of the church and found that during a certain month, two thirds of the support of our church came through his company or through those working for him.

About two weeks after this man had gotten saved, I was shaving one morning and getting ready to downtown to buy some groceries and go to the post office to pick up our mail.

While I was shaving, the Spirit of God spoke to me, on the inside of me, in my spirit. It wasn't audible, but it was the inward Voice of the Holy Spirit, and He said to me, "Before you go to town, go out to _____ 's house and pray for him" (talking about the businessman who had just gotten saved).

The Lord said, "He got mad on the job, lost his temper, and cursed. I want you to go restore him." So I said to my wife, "The Lord told me I've got to go see _____. The Lord just told me he lost his temper on the job, and he's home sick in bed over it. The Lord told me to go see him and restore him."

Oretha said, "Go ahead then. The errands can wait. We're not in any hurry." So I finished shaving and started putting on my tie when I heard a car drive up in front of the parsonage. I looked out the window and saw this man's wife.

She came in and said, "Oh, Brother and Sister Hagin, please don't tell _____ that I came here. He'll have a fit if he knew. But he got mad on the job and lost his temper. He said he was so mad, he didn't remember it, but some of the men said he cursed. He told me, 'If I did, I don't know it.'

"But now he says, 'I've backslidden. I'm never going to church anymore.' He had injured his back working awhile ago. And now that back injury's come back on him, and he's home in bed sick. Will you go see him?

"But don't tell him I came by here. If he asks you, 'Have you been talking to my wife?' I don't know what to tell you to do."

"Well, I know what I'm going to do," I said. "You just ask my wife. I told her less than 10 minutes ago that the Lord spoke to me and told me to go over there and see your husband. So I can tell him truthfully that the Lord sent me, because He did."

So I went to the man's house. His wife told me where he was, so I went around to a side door and knocked. He hollered, "Come in," but when I opened the door and looked in and he saw me, he jerked the bed covers up over his head. He was embarrassed, bless his heart.

But you remember he was just two weeks old in the Lord. I'll tell you, sometimes we folks who are older in the Lord forget what it's like to be newly saved. Somebody gets saved Sunday night, and we expect them to be living as good a separated and holy life as we are now (but when we first got saved, we didn't do that in our own lives either!).

And so he jerked the cover up over his head. I just got on my knees beside the bed, and I had a time doing it, but I finally managed to pull the covers off his head!

I wasn't but a boy then, just 27 or 28 years old. This man was in his forties. But I took him in my arms and began to cry with him. He was crying, and I just began to weep with him.

I said, "Brother _____, I was shaving, the Lord spoke to me and sent me over here. We're not going to let the devil have you. You may have missed it, but we're not going to let the devil have you."

"Oh, Brother Hagin," he said, "I'm just so embarrassed. I did get mad, and I lost my temper. I know that. But I don't remember anything I said. I was so mad, I don't know what I said. And some of the men said I cursed."

A person can get so mad he doesn't know what he's doing. I know—I've been there, but not since I was a Christian. I've got as much temper now as I ever had before, but I control it. I've never let it get away from me since I've been a Christian.

Before I was a Christian, I could get so mad at someone, I'd knock him in the head before he could say scat! And I'd get so mad, I didn't know what I was doing sometimes. I've been just that mad before.

"Well," this man said, "I had that back injury, and it seemed like I was over it pretty good. But it's come back on me, and I'm in misery and pain."

This man was a genuine spiritual baby. I laid my hand on his back and said, "Dear God, now You love him, and I know You do. I know he's failed. I know he's sinned, but he's ashamed of it and has repented of it. Lord, just prove to him right now that You love him. Heal his back."

And I remember the man looked at me, and just as fast as you could snap your fingers, he was healed. He looked startled and jumped like you'd shocked him with electricity. He said, "You know, it's all gone. The pain left." He was instantly perfectly well.

He broke down and began to cry and said, "You mean the Lord loves me enough to heal me?"

I said, "He loves you enough, and He's restored you." Well, this man came on back to church. We didn't let the devil have him.

I had to go one other time about a month or so later to restore this man. He got mad again on the job. But I didn't have to go anymore after that.

But, after all, what do you expect out of a baby? They can't do too much for themselves. Somebody's got to carry them. We're going to have to give account unto God for what we've done with the babies who've been born in our midst into the Kingdom of God.

The second time the Lord spoke to me to go and restore this man, the minute it happened and he lost his temper at work, the Lord spoke to my heart and told me what had happened.

I went out and restored him, and 25 years later, he was on the church board and working for God. He was paying his tithes and living right.

I could carry this man on my own faith while he was a genuine spiritual baby. But let me show you something about those who have been babies for years and have not grown spiritually.

I had a deacon in my church who lived close to this man I'd restored twice. This deacon was the head deacon. He'd always testify that he'd been saved and filled with the Holy Ghost for nearly 30 years.

This deacon was nearly 30 years old in the Lord, and he came to me one day just a crying.

He said to me, "I told somebody, 'Brother Hagin doesn't love me. I saw him twice in the last two months out there at Brother _____'s house, and he never comes to see me.'"

I said, "Yes, and I'm not coming either. You're a big baby. You get up and testify in church that you've been saved and filled with the Holy Ghost for nearly 30 years. You don't need anybody to visit you! You're thirty years old in the Lord—you ought to be out visiting others.

"Brother _____ is a baby Christian. He needed somebody to help him. You don't need anybody to help you. You ought to be helping me take care of the spiritual babies. But instead, you want to be babied yourself.

"So just go ahead and bawl if you want to," I continued. "I'm not going to sympathize with you or have one bit of compassion on you. You don't need it.

"And while I'm at it, I want to say something else to you. If you don't quit running around sticking your nose into other people's business, you're going to draw back one of these days, and you're not going to have a nose. Somebody's going to cut it off!"

I didn't mean someone was going to literally cut off his nose. But sometimes folks get the idea that God sort of ordained them and called them to run everybody else's business in the church!

God Wants Us to Grow Up Spiritually

I just told this deacon the truth. And he appreciated it. Actually, he got a little huffy right then, but he thought about it, and he came back and thanked me. He shook hands with me and said, "Brother Hagin, thank you. One thing I like about you is I understand you. I see what you were talking about.

"You're exactly, one-hundred percent right," he continued, "and I'm one hundred percent wrong. I'm going to get out there and help you a little bit more. I don't need anybody to visit me. I ought to be visiting some of the babies and seeing about them and helping you out. I see that. And not only that, but I see I've tried to poke my nose in too many people's business around here. So I'm quitting it right now."

You see, as long as people are really genuine spiritual babies, you can carry them with your faith and get things from God for them. It's the easiest thing in the world to get somebody healed who's a new Christian.

Not only that, but it's comparatively easy, as a usual thing, to get Christians healed who have never heard about divine healing. They haven't been taught. So very often you can make your faith work for them. But God expects a little bit more out of those who know about divine healing and have been taught the Word.

I remember when my wife and I first married, she was Methodist and knew nothing about divine healing. She hadn't been taught. I'd learned about divine healing on the bed of sickness as a Baptist boy. So about a month after we were married, cold weather began to set in. We'd had some cool spells already, but the first real norther blew in about a month after we were married.

Oretha began to have a sore throat. She said, "I've got to go and have my throat mopped out." That's what they did back then. They didn't have any miracle drugs, so the doctor would mop your throat out.

Oretha said the doctor had wanted to operate and take her tonsils out a time or two before. He said they were bad and needed to come out. But each time he wanted to operate, she was running a little fever, so they couldn't put her under the anesthesia.

Oretha said, "I'll have a bad throat all winter. I do every year. When the first real cold spell comes, I get a bad throat, and I have it all winter. Even though I go periodically and have it mopped out and do everything I know to do, it stays bad all winter."

I thought, "This would be a good opportunity to start teaching her about faith." We'd been married about a month. And I remembered Mark 11:23.

Sometimes people think the Bible will work for you if you've got some kind of a feeling. But God's Word is just as true when you feel like it's true as when you feel like it isn't true. It's still true, and still works.

Sometimes people think you can sort of work yourself up into faith some way or another. But you can't. Or some people think faith will work if you feel some kind of a flash. But that's not so either. When I used my faith for Oretha, I didn't have a cold flash, or a hot flash, or any kind of flash. In fact, I never felt a thing that I know of. I just knew that Mark 11:23 is truth and that it works.

It works regardless of how you feel. Don't base your faith on your feelings. Base it on the Word.

When Mark 11:23 Will Work for Others

I didn't pray for my wife, because I knew that whosoever shall *say* and not doubt in his heart, but shall believe that those things which he saith shall come to pass, he'll have whatsoever he saith. I just said to her, "No, we'll not go have your throat mopped out. That chronic throat trouble will leave you and will never come back."

Well, it left her, in all the years that have come and gone since, it's never come back!

But, you see, I couldn't do that for her later. She had to do it for herself. She learned that Mark 11:23 worked. Then it was up to her to exercise and develop her faith. And, praise God, she has.

I had the greatest time in my life demonstrating to all my kin folks that Mark 11:23 worked.

Once my uncle asked for prayer. He and his family weren't even saved. His youngest daughter was in the hospital, and the doctor said she was dying.

Mamma had called me and said, "Uncle ____ wants you to pray for Sarah. She's dying." The best doctors around had given her up.

Sarah was a grown girl, but she was still her daddy's baby girl.

I thought this would be a good opportunity to show them Mark 11:23 works. They didn't know about Mark 11:23. They weren't even saved.

I said, "Mamma, when Aunt ____ calls you back, tell her to tell Uncle ____ that I said Sarah will live and not die."

"Oh, son," Mamma said, "do you think so?"

I said, "No, I don't *think* so—I *know* so."

"Well," she said, "have you heard from the Lord?"

I said, "Yeah, I sure have."

"Well, that's fine then. Praise the Lord."

Mamma knew the Lord would tell me things at times, and so she was satisfied with that.

I continued: "Yeah, I've heard from the Lord, all right, and Sarah will live and not die.

"Well, praise the Lord," she said. "That's fine then."

I continued: "Yeah, I heard from the Lord—Mark 11:23!"

"Oh?" she asked.

People put more emphasis on some kind of manifestation than they do the written Word of God. Don't ever do that! I said, don't do that! Put the emphasis on the *Word*! In everything, put the *Word* first.

I said, "Yes, Mamma, I heard from Heaven." Sure I did. I heard from God, because in Mark 11:23, Jesus said, *"whosoever shall SAY."*

"Now you tell Aunt _____ what I said."

"Well, do you suppose it'll work, son?"

I thought, "Bless her heart." I said, "Sure it'll work."

If you work Mark 11:23—if you'll act on that scripture—it'll work! It's the Word that does the work, not *you*! You're not going to do it; the *Word* is going to do the work.

That's where a lot of people miss it. They think they're the ones who are going to have to do the work.

Mamma had asked me, "Do you suppose it'll work?"

I told her, "*I'm* not going to heal Sarah. *God's* going to do it. All I'm going to do is do what the Word said. So you tell them that I said Sarah will live and not die and that she'll be all right."

"Well, I sure hope so."

"Well," I said, "you tell them exactly what I told you. Will you do it? Repeat it for me so I'll know you got it right." So Mamma repeated it for me.

After I hung up the phone, I went my way. My mind kept saying, "You've put yourself out on a limb. Now they're all going to find out what a fake you are."

Did the devil ever tell you that? Did he ever tell you, *Your faith is not going to work. Your kinfolks are going to find out that there's nothing to all this faith business you've been preaching all these years.*

That's what he said to me. But I just didn't pay any attention to my head. Praise God, the first person I could get to, I got to talking to them about what Mark 11:23 says and how it works.

I had to make a little trip with a friend of mine, and when we got back, I called Mamma. "Did you tell them what I told you to tell them?"

"Yeah," she said, "and after I told them, it wasn't thirty minutes until Aunt _____ called back and said, 'I told _____ what Ken said. Sarah was lying there in the Intensive Care Unit with three doctors gathered around her, shaking their heads. They said she'd never come out it — she wouldn't live.

"But just after I told them what you said, within 10 minutes, she came out of it. She just suddenly opened her eyes and was all right! And now she's perfectly fine.'"

I said, "I knew it all the time."

"How'd you know it?" Mamma asked.

"Mark 11:23 said so."

Just by acting on Mark 11:23, I made that scripture work in every family among my relatives, and I brought the supernatural power of God into their lives. But then after that, I never could do it again.

You Can't Carry Others on
Your Own Faith Indefinitely

You see, by me acting on Mark 11:23 and making it work for them, they had concrete evidence that it worked. Then when they needed prayer, they'd come back to me the next time, and I couldn't carry them on my faith. God expected a little more out of them this time. He wanted them to do a little bit—at least to agree with me.

You can't always make your faith work for other folks. It's not right that you carry people indefinitely with your faith. It's not right that you carry people spiritually any more than it's right that you carry people naturally.

It's not normal for parents to carry their children all their lives. Those children are eventually going to have to get out on their own.

In the same way, the time's coming when God's going to say, "You put that big youngun' down and let him walk for himself." (You might as well listen to me — I'm telling you the truth!)

But this is not bad news; it's good news. God wants you to grow up spiritually and develop in faith for yourself. You need to experience for yourself the goodness of God's Word and His faithfulness to perform it on your behalf if you'll believe it. Then you can move mountains in your life and be a blessing to others. You *have* mountain-moving faith!

Prayer of Salvation
to Receive Jesus as Savior

Dear Heavenly Father,

I come to You in the Name of Jesus.

Your Word says, *"The one who comes to Me I will by no means cast out"* (John 6:37 NKJV). I know You won't cast me out. You take me in, and I thank You for that.

You said in Your Word, *"Whoever calls on the name of the Lord shall be saved"* (Romans 10:13 NKJV). I am calling on Your Name, and I know You have saved me.

You also said, *"If you confess with your mouth the Lord Jesus and believe in your heart that God has raised Him from the dead, you will be saved. For with the heart one believes unto righteousness, and with the mouth confession is made unto salvation"* (Romans 10:9–10 NKJV). I believe in my heart Jesus Christ is the Son of God. I believe He died on the cross and was raised from the dead to pay the penalty for my sins. I confess Him as my Lord.

Because Your Word says that *"with the heart one believes unto righteousness,"*—and I do believe with my heart—I have now become the righteousness of God in Christ (2 Corinthians 5:21). I am now saved!

Thank You, Lord!

Signed _____

Date _____

Rhema Word Partner Club

WORKING *together* TO REACH THE WORLD!

People. Power. Purpose.

Have you ever dropped a stone into water? Small waves rise up at the point of impact and travel in all directions. It's called a ripple effect. That's the kind of impact Christians are meant to have in this world—the kind of impact that the Rhema family is producing in the earth today.

The Rhema Word Partner Club links Christians with a shared interest in reaching people with the Gospel and the message of faith in God.

Together we are reaching across generations, cultures, and nations to spread the Good News of Jesus Christ to every corner of the earth.

To join us in reaching the world,
visit **rhema.org/wpc** or call **1-866-312-0972**.

Always on.

For the latest news and information on products, media, podcasts, study resources, and special offers, visit us online 24 hours a day.

rhema.org

Free Subscription!

Call now to receive a free subscription to *The Word of Faith* magazine from Kenneth Hagin Ministries. Receive encouragement and spiritual refreshment from . . .

- *Faith-building articles from Kenneth W. Hagin, Lynette Hagin, Craig W. Hagin, Denise Hagin Burns, and others*

- *"Timeless Teaching" from the archives of Kenneth E. Hagin*

- *Feature articles on prayer and healing*

- *Testimonies of salvation, healing, and deliverance*

- *Children's activity page*

- *Updates on Rhema Bible Training College, Rhema Bible Church, and other outreaches of Kenneth Hagin Ministries*

Rhema
Correspondence Bible School

The Rhema Correspondence Bible School is a home Bible study course that can help you in your everyday life!

This course of study has been designed with you in mind, providing practical teaching on prayer, faith, healing, Spirit-led living, and much more to help you live a victorious Christian life!

Flexible
Enroll any time: choose your topic of study;
study at your own pace!

Affordable

Profitable

"The Lord has blessed me through a Rhema Correspondence Bible School graduate. . . . He witnessed to me 15 years ago, and the Lord delivered me from drugs and alcohol. I was living on the streets and then in somebody's tool shed. Now I lead a victorious and blessed life! I now am a graduate of Rhema Correspondence Bible School too! I own a beautiful home. I have a beautiful wife and two children who also love the Lord. The Lord allows me to preach whenever my pastor is out of town. I am on the board of directors at my church and at the Christian school. Thank you, and God bless you and your ministry!"

—D.J., Lusby, Maryland

"Thank you for continually offering Rhema Correspondence Bible School. The eyes of my understanding have been enlightened greatly through the Word of God through having been enrolled in RCBS. My life has forever been changed."

—M.R., Princeton, N.C.

For enrollment information and a course listing, call today!
1-888-28-FAITH (1-888-283-2484)
rhema.org/rcbs